101

THINGS CANADIANS
SHOULD KNOW ABOUT
CANADA

101

THINGS CANADIANS
SHOULD KNOW ABOUT
CANADA

EDITED BY RUDYARD GRIFFITHS

KEY PORTER BOOKS

Library and Archives Canada Cataloguing in Publication

101 things Canadians should know about Canada / edited by Rudyard Griffiths.

ISBN 978-1-55263-995-5

1. Canada—Miscellanea. 2. Canada—History—Miscellanea.
I. Griffiths, Rudyard. II. Title. III. Title: One hundred one things Canadians should know about Canada.

FC60.O54 2008   971   C2008-902210-6

The publisher gratefully acknowledges the support of the Canada Council for the Arts and the Ontario Arts Council for its publishing program. We acknowledge the support of the Government of Ontario through the Ontario Media Development Corporation's Ontario Book Initiative.

We acknowledge the financial support of the Government of Canada through the Book Publishing Industry Development Program (BPIDP) for our publishing activities.

Key Porter Books Limited
Six Adelaide Street East, Tenth Floor
Toronto, Ontario
Canada M5C 1H6
www.keyporter.com

Text design: Marijke Friesen
Electronic formatting: Alison Carr
Printed and bound in Canada

08 09 10 11 12 5 4 3 2

CONTENTS

Introduction

Canadians have long thought of their country as a study in difference. We take great pride in our national accomplishments in the worlds of sports, business, and science, but we also maintain strong regional identities based on language, geography, or, in the case of Canada's Aboriginal peoples, racial ancestry. We see ourselves as a northern nation even though nine in ten Canadians live within 160 kilometres of the U.S. border. We champion institutions and values we share in common, such as peacekeeping, health care, and respect for each other's differences, yet many of our values also underscore, and sometimes exacerbate, our differences along ethnic, regional, and linguistic lines.

We see ourselves predominantly as a polyglot and restless nation---a country that is simultaneously comfortable with the idea that our mishmash sense of ourselves is our shared identity but also prone to worrying about what binds us together as Canadians, today and into the future.

101 Things Canadians Should Know About Canada is the Dominion Institute's playful rebuttal of the notion that we are a nation of contrasts, a country always searching for a consensus as to what Canada "is."

The idea for this book was born in 2007 when we sat down with our friends at the polling firm Ipsos Reid to try to figure out how similar, or not, average Canadians' opinions are about the people, places, events, accomplishments, and symbols that they think define the country.

Then, with the support of Citizenship and Immigration Canada, we surveyed over 3,000 people nationwide, making our study the largest of its kind. We also polled immigrants, educators, and members of the country's highest civil honour, the Order of Canada. By including these sub-groups, we could find out if Canadians' sense of what defines their country was influenced by factors other than region, income, education, and gender.

Leaving no stone unturned, we also created a bilingual website—www.101things.ca— where Canadians could log on and vote for the one thing they thought was missing from the master list of 101 people, places, events, accomplishments, and symbols as generated by our Ipsos Reid study.

At the time of publication, some 4,000 online ballots had been cast for the 102nd "thing," with Aboriginal Canadians being the most popular choice.

What did we discover after conducting this unprecedented study? And, more important, what might you learn from reading this book?

In this great sprawling country of ours, we found that whether you are a man or a woman, young or old, from Trois-Rivières or Tuktoyaktuk, from a family that has lived in Canada for four years or 400 years, the top ten things that you think define the country will include six or more items that are also on the lists of each of your fellow 33 million Canucks. Neat, eh?

Even in Québec, which the rest of Canada might well assume is off marching to its own cultural drumbeat, survey participants ranked the Maple Leaf, the Canadarm, the Beaver, Parliament Hill, and Canada Day as their top five choices for what defines Canada—all iconic symbols that featured prominently in the top ten lists of Canadians from coast to coast to coast.

There were also striking similarities between the top ten lists for immigrants and for the general public. Immigrants not only chose the Maple Leaf as the country's defining overall symbol but also nine of the ten places, events, heroes, and accomplishments that constituted the general public's top ten list. These results suggest that Canada enjoys a collective identity that is every bit as effective at absorbing newcomers as the melting pot of our southern neighbours in the United States.

Interestingly, the real outliers—the one group whose sense of what defines Canada diverged most from that of the general public—were the 300 or so members of the Order of Canada who took part in the survey.

The recipients of Canada's highest civil honour ranked the discovery of insulin as the country's defining feature, an achievement that ranked fifteenth overall on the general public's list. Number eleven on their list was the Battle of the Plains of Abraham, an event that was ranked thirty-first by the general public. Not surprisingly, Ottawa appears on the Order of Canada's top ten list, though it is conspicuously absent from the general public's.

To put it mildly, there was a cultural chasm between what the country's elites think defines Canada versus the opinion of the general population and newcomers.

In the final analysis, *101 Things Canadians Should Know About Canada* shows that we are not, as we are often told, a disparate nation made up of ornery regions, cloistered ethnic groups, and aggrieved linguistic communities. Instead, we are a people who enjoy and benefit from a set of widely shared understandings about the fundamentals of a common Canadian identity.

I hope the publication of this book, and the excellent write-ups of the list of the 101 "things" by a star-studded cast of Canadians, gives all of us—including our schools, museums, and governments—the confidence to start discussing and debating the rich body of knowledge and opinion we share in common, as opposed to what divides us.

Rudyard Griffiths, Editor
Erin, Ontario

1 The Maple Leaf
Tomson Highway

I'm from subarctic Manitoba, where there are no maple trees of any kind. In southern Manitoba, yes, they do have maples, Manitoba maples, that is, not sugar maples, the kind whose leaves turn bright red in the fall. In the far north, where I come from, among trees deciduous we have only birch, poplar, and willow, trees whose leaves turn yellow and orange and brown in autumn, just not red.

Later in my life, I ended up at the University of Western Ontario in London to study music and (for me) that most foreign of languages: English. I arrived in eastern Canada in late summer, and that fall, on one of those note-perfect, crisp, sun-splashed mornings, I found myself walking to the university campus across this park, a route I normally did not take.

So there I was walking. And walking and walking and thinking and thinking, blind to passing people, blind to passing traffic, the only thing I saw the thoughts jostling for attention inside my mind. All of a sudden, I found myself standing in front of this gigantic, this magnificent, this incredibly tall sugar maple. For one born near the treeline, that's what it was: tall. Its leaves were so bright in their redness it almost hurt the eyes to look at it. And because not a cloud marred a clear blue sky, sunlight fell on it undiluted, uninterrupted. And there was a breeze that seeped through the complex filigree of foliage in such a way that the leaves trembled, shuddered, shimmered. And whispered.

I was transfixed. I had never in my life seen such a vision. And it was at that precise moment—at age twenty-two, some thirty years ago—that I became, for life, an Ontarian. I've been here ever since and will probably die here, at this cottage in northern Ontario surrounded by the shimmer and the whisper of fire-engine-red sugar maple leaves.

2 Hockey
Dave Bidini

Explaining hockey to Canadians is like explaining water to a river. 99 plus 66 minus 77 divided by 4 gives you 7 or 9 but never 3. Paul Henderson was born in a sleigh. Cyclone Taylor's mom invented the shoulder pad. Gordie Howe once lifted an opposing player to his feet by embedding two fingers in his nostrils. Bryan Trottier's childhood linemate was his dog. Garnet Bailey was killed by terrorists. Dick Redmond regrets that he never gigged with Boston. Was Pavel Bure Lukachenko's stooge? Opposing fans threw steak knives at the Gumper. Clare Alexander was a milkman. Phil Esposito broke his mother's heart (whenever he scored on Tony). Foster Hewitt's mantra: flow and anticipate. The Rocket coached the Nordiques for one game, then quit. Was Red Kelly the greatest player ever? Synthesizers have no place in hockey. The Ducks is a friendly name. Why must Toronto fans care? Bathgate's curved blade was the first, possibly. Pucks were once made out of chocolate and Christmas was better back then. Trevor Linden made Lorna cry. Gilbert Perreault, and other opposing players you cheered for. Mario on John Casey; the Silver Seven on the Klondike. The Igloo, starring Wally Boyer. Bugsy stopped talking and I never pressed him. Got 'em. Need 'em? Garter belts strapped frilly to an angry man. The Spectrum, where fans were hairy, especially the women. Chiclets. The Flower. The Moustache. Hockey Lives Here, Vladimir Dzurilla was a refrigerator repair man; he wore a white mask made of bones. The Smoke Eaters of Trail. Federov and Salming and the first player from France. Helmeted. Brazen. Cold and colder. My feet used to hurt, but now they do not.

The Canadian Flag
Todd Babiak

In 1956, Lester B. Pearson, then minister of external affairs, helped broker a peace deal between Egypt and a coalition of British, French, and Israeli forces, effectively ending the Suez Crisis. He won the Nobel Peace Prize for his efforts and, like all Canadians who are recognized abroad, Pearson instantly became a national hero. In 1963, he became prime minister, leading a minority Liberal government.

Pearson was haunted by Egypt's contention, during the Suez Crisis, that an apparently neutral country—Canada—carried an image of the Union Jack on its flag. The Red Ensign, the "Canadian flag" since 1870, was not only problematic for Canada's international brand, it was also unpopular in Québec.

In 1964, Pearson's government set out to adopt a new, wholly Canadian flag. The prime minister had his favourite design, but so did everyone else. A spirited "Great Flag Debate" ensued. The Conservatives, led by John Diefenbaker, wanted to keep the Red Ensign. Pearson himself preferred a red-on-white three-leaf maple design, with blue bars on the outside, known as the "Pearson Pennant."

An all-party committee was struck, and its members considered over 3,500 possibilities. It came down to a battle between the Pennant, with its suspiciously un-Canadian blue bars, and the design we now know as "the Maple Leaf," created by history professor George Stanley. The committee adopted Stanley's design and, after a lengthy filibuster by the pugnacious Diefenbaker and the Conservatives, Pearson invoked closure on the debate and the divided House of Commons voted. The Canadian flag was born on December 15, 1964.

Over the last forty years, Canadian (and even some American) backpackers in Europe have ironed the flag onto their gear in order to seem quiet, polite, apologetic, and humble. In recent years, Canadians have eschewed symbolic understatement. Large Maple Leaf tattoos, T-shirts, umbrellas, and tchotchkes are increasingly common in Canada and wherever Canadians congregate around the world.

4 The Beaver
Tomson Highway

There is nothing quite like the experience of sitting on the deck of your summer cottage, the lake at your feet mirror-smooth and flawless, stretching off into infinity (and if not into infinity then at least across the lake to that stand of sugar maples a half-kilometre from where you are sitting), and the silence is so perfect that you swear you can hear the movement of ants in that little pile of sand not ten yards off. And you're sitting there and thinking how fortunate you are to have been born in a land so awesome when, all of a sudden, you hear a splash. And your gaze is pulled to the ripple that has broken the glass-smooth surface that is Trout Lake—or Bear Lake or Lake Misty Maskimoot—and you realize, again (because this, of course, has happened a thousand times before), that it's your beaver playing silly games with you, slapping its fat tail in the water and then diving under, forever in search of that scrumptious shoot, that tasty morsel. And then the little critter gainfully resurfaces to continue its journey, off the other way to where its house stands, its scaly little nose poking out of the water like a mini periscope, slicing water as it goes, the ripples that it makes fanning out and out and out, not a single sound to mar them, just rippling silence. And you know you're home, home where you were born, home where you belong.

Even though the beaver can be found in other countries, such as the U.S., France, even Argentina, it still seems uniquely Canadian. That's OUR animal. She's on our nickel. To us, *amisk*—"beaver" in Cree, my mother tongue, stress on the second syllable—means "Canada."

5 The Canadarm
David Eddie

It is as long as two telephone poles and has six joints, roughly corresponding to the joints of a human arm, controlling the "roll," "yaw," and "pitch" of the arm. The word "Canada," along with a red maple leaf, is proudly tattooed on its long, stringy white "bicep," and another appears on its "forearm."

Its real name is the Shuttle Remote Manipulator System (SRMS), but we all know it as the Canadarm, and it's Canada's most significant contribution to the space program. While it may seem a minor contribution to some, it is a crucial, subtle, and beautiful piece of engineering.

NASA took a chance trusting one of the most important aspects of its new shuttle program to a relatively untested Canadian engineering team in 1975, and it has paid off in spades. Among its impressive attributes is the ability to capture a free-floating payload in a zero-gravity environment. It is extraordinarily sensitive and can be moved slowly over a distance of a few millimetres to capture a tiny object, or very quickly across a distance of several metres.

It has been used for everything from knocking ice off the fuselage of the Orbiter to fixing the Hubble Space Telescope. And it has been instrumental in space assembly, including that of the International Space Station.

Following the Space Shuttle *Columbia* disaster in 2003, in which the shuttle disintegrated on re-entry, resulting in the death of all seven souls on board, the arm has been used to check hull integrity on re-entry.

Over the course of more than fifty missions and after nearly 7,000 orbits around the earth, it has never—not once—malfunctioned.

The "arm in space" is one of Canada's greatest engineering achievements. And it's an expression of the best of Canada's soul: not flashy, not ostentatious, but useful, dependable, and willing to reach out and lend a strong but sensitive hand wherever one is needed, no matter how far-flung.

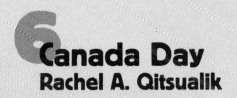

6 Canada Day
Rachel A. Qitsualik

If there is anything emblematic of the Canadian spirit, it is the July 1st anniversary of Confederation, now known as Canada Day; emblematic not because of festivity, but rather because of the evolution of the holiday itself. If one tracks the development of Canada Day, one tracks the birth and maturation of Canadian nationalism.

That "birth" might be said to be the 1868 proclamation by Governor General Lord Monck, urging Canadians to celebrate . . . well, Canadian-ness. If we are to go by the records of the years following that proclamation, it was met with the sounds of crickets and snores. This is not surprising, considering that "Canadians" of that era considered themselves British, the French had their own distinct culture, and the Aboriginal peoples were still wondering why they weren't allowed to live on their land anymore.

Even the federal government did not celebrate the suggested holiday until 1917, and then it was simply to commemorate the golden anniversary of Confederation. Actual Dominion Day celebrations, with fireworks and parades, were not held on Parliament Hill until 1958 (a whopping ninety years after Monck), giving us an idea of how long it takes for Canadians to build enthusiasm for new concepts.

We can thank television (the sixties) and a general loosening of Ottawa's purse strings (the eighties) for Canada Day as we now know it. With money at last doled out to provinces and territories to encourage local celebrations, Dominion Day began to assume its contemporary shape; in other words, the "folk" at last embraced it, calling it "Canada Day" (adopted officially in 1982) and imbuing it with true national texture. Today, Canada Day is in fullest bloom, having assumed a beautiful and valuable multicultural theme, and serving as the only venue through which urban centres annually see Chinese food served next to Greek souvlaki.

7 Peacekeeping
Rick Mercer

The idea of peacekeeping is a simple one—a country's military should not only defend its own interests and security, but also has an international obligation to prevent war. And the force best suited to ensure that ceasefire agreements are carried out is a neutral and multi-national one.

Canadians have a unique ownership of the idea: Lester B. Pearson, Canada's fourteenth prime minister, is recognized worldwide as the father of modern peacekeeping.

In 1956, the world watched as a terrifying crisis developed at the Suez Canal: Egypt had seized the canal, leading to an invasion by Britain and France. The conflict not only pitted the interests of the United States against those of the United Kingdom, but involved enemy nations from the Middle East and the added threat of Soviet intervention. It was Pearson, then a diplomat, who suggested that a neutral United Nations Emergency Force be created in the Suez to "keep the borders at peace while a political settlement is being worked out."

The UN followed Pearson's lead, and a neutral peacekeeping force, which included Canadian soldiers, was created. It kept the peace, thus allowing time for diplomacy to work to end tensions.

Since then, Canada has taken part in more peacekeeping missions than any other country. And while all of Canada has benefited from our reputation as peacekeepers, the work and sacrifice has fallen on the shoulders of the more than 110,000 Canadians who have donned the blue berets and helmets of peacekeeping forces to serve in zones of conflict around the world.

Their service to Canada and the world was memorialized in 1992 with the unveiling of the Peacekeeping Monument in Ottawa, the only such monument in the world.

8 Pierre Elliott Trudeau
J. L. Granatstein

When Pierre Trudeau died on September 28, 2000, the public response in Canada was unprecedented. No other politician, not even Macdonald or Laurier, had ever received such accolades, such a nationalistic outpouring of grief, though, in truth, it was much more pronounced outside Québec. For a politician and thinker whose stock-in-trade was anti-nationalism, this was surely extraordinary.

Trudeau deeply mistrusted Québec *nationalisme*, and the separatists and intellectuals there in turn hated him. He also worried about the excesses of English-Canadian nationalism, but he curtailed foreign investment, for example, which only fed it. Above all, Trudeau feared that nationalism could override individual freedoms, and after a long struggle he managed to entrench the Canadian Charter of Rights and Freedoms into the Constitution that he patriated in 1982. Ironically, many commentators on both the left and right dislike his Charter, seeing it as fostering judge-made law and helping to Americanize Canada. Far more people, however, applaud its tough protection of individual freedoms.

A controversial lawyer and academic, Trudeau entered politics in 1965 to help counter the rise of separatism in Québec. Three years later, he was a charismatic prime minister, riding a nationalist wave. But in October 1970, Trudeau, the civil libertarian, used the army to crush Québec terrorism, and some of the glow disappeared. Nor was he a good manager, his free-spending governments racking up huge deficits while starving the military. He fought with American administrations about Cuba and Cold War policy, and he cozied up to the Soviets. His critics forgive him none of these things.

Yet Trudeau, perfectly bilingual, debonair, and highly intelligent, embodied the characteristics to which Canadians aspired. He had style and exuded sex appeal, and his intellect enabled him to make a mark on the global stage. Historians do not (yet) rank him among the great prime ministers for his almost sixteen years in power. Canadians, without doubt, do.

Health Care
Christopher Moore

The historian Michael Bliss writes that as religious faith declined in the twentieth century, the life expectancy of Canadians also declined: from eternity to a hundred years or less. Is that why we now make a "sacred trust" of the public health care system, which has become our chief protection against our fears of disease, incapacity ... and death?

Until the 1950s, Canadians got medical treatment with cold cash, private insurance, or charity. In the prosperous 1950s and 1960s, Canadians who had endured the grim 1930s and the wartime sacrifices of the 1940s, developed both the mood and the means for what they came to call "the social safety net." That meant better public services, old-age pensions, unemployment insurance, legal aid, union bargaining rights ... and universal medical coverage.

Two politicians and a judge stand out in the making of medicare. In 1962, Saskatchewan premier Tommy Douglas introduced Canada's first universal medical-care insurance program. Judge Emmett Hall, also from Saskatchewan, led the royal commission (1964–65) that charted a plan for nationwide medicare. And it was prime minister Lester B. Pearson's government that negotiated federal-provincial agreements and saw the legislation passed—in a minority Parliament—that led to Canada-wide medicare in 1966.

Health care is still a provincial responsibility. It is the provinces that provide medical facilities and run the insurance programs that pay for medical care. In exchange for financial contributions, the federal government requires that each province's medical care meet uniform tests for availability, universality, comprehensiveness, portability, and administrative efficiency.

Canadians' ever-growing appetite for medical services creates problems of rising costs, rationing of services, and individuals wishing to "opt out." Governments and the courts struggle endlessly to square the circle: to design a system that will be unlimited yet affordable, and still respect individual rights. Yet, as much as we argue about medicare, it has taken less than fifty years for most Canadians to see it as one of the fundamental benefits of being Canadian.

10 Niagara Falls
Dave Bidini

Way back in ancient times, a great hole opened along the Canada–U.S. border, and before you knew it, there were wax museums and tents with bearded ladies and twenty-five-cent rides for the kiddies and hot dog stands lining the thoroughfares around the great hole, which saw multitudinous gallons of fresh, frothy water poured into it over cliffs where, occasionally, one of our fabulously unhinged stood dressed in hot red or black tie or superhero blue, weighing their daredevil's heart before hopefully (and a mite foolishly) plummeting in barrels and other dirigibilia towards the swirling lake below, hoping to avoid the slowly cruising vessel that has appeared in wedding rolls and video since before God was a cowboy—the blue and white *Maid of the Mist* touring ship—slattern to the unruly eighth wonder of the world and magnet for starry-eyed runaways, Punjabi tourists, misguided touts, and stricken gamblers hoping to rid themselves of those sins of the velvet incurred just blocks away in the gambling emporia that now dominate the cityscape, whereas before there were only the great cascading falls and trees poking perpendicular out of a jagged rock face, which, in the days before neon billboards and circus freaks and superheroes was a good enough reason to seek Lourdes at home, magnificence nearby, the chance to touch the Earth's greatness, if only for an annual heated pool and colour television weekend, breakfast included.

11 The Rockies/
The Rocky Mountains
Michelle Berry

I remember the first time I flew over the Rocky Mountains. It was 1975 and I was seven years old. We were new to Canada, a homesick family going back east to spend Christmas with our relatives. I had my first camera and one roll of film. Aiming out the plane window, I took almost my whole roll of pictures of the sunset as it lit up the Rocky Mountains peeking out of the clouds. Everything was a vivid pink and yellow, indigo, blue and snow white. I got the occasional shot of window frame, or of my brother's head, or of the sky. If I close my eyes now, I can still see those majestic mountains and feel the turbulence as the plane passed over. I can still remember the effect of that great, huge, colourful beauty passing below.

The Rockies stretch from northern British Columbia to New Mexico and have a rich, and sometimes brutal, history. From Native tribes to explorers, from fur traders to gold prospectors, from tourists to sports enthusiasts, the Rocky Mountains have seen many people come and go, each drawn to something mysterious or desirable. The Rockies are a natural wall between eastern and western Canada. And it's accepted wisdom that the people who live west of the Rockies are different from those who live east. This huge mountain range blocking easy travel has perhaps created a difference in perspective, a different culture and way of life. Our environment defines us, after all.

Over the years I have flown back and forth across the Rockies many times. Each time they were as staggeringly beautiful as the first. Each time I wanted to push aside the person in the window seat and take more pictures. I recently found that first roll I took and, interestingly, the pictures were black and white. The colour I remember is there, though. I can still see it in my mind's eye.

12 Wayne Gretzky
Dave Bidini

This is Wayne Gretzky as a person. In 1991, I covered the Canada Cup for the *Village Voice*. In the dressing room after a Canadian victory (they were all victories back then), we surrounded 99 as he sat at his stall in the dressing room. At Wayne's knee was a small, nebbish American sportswriter, who wouldn't have known Dale Hawerchuk from Dale Evans, taking notes. After getting his requisite quote, the reporter pushed his pencil—pointy side up—through the rings of his notepad and left the scene. As he did, the pencil lead tore into the most famous leg in hockey (though not the most famous knee; that would be Bobby Orr's), shredding the Great One's trousers. Were he you or I, he might have risen from his position and throttled the ink-stained pinhead, outraged with his carelessness. Instead, he rubbed his hind and looked forlorn, then proceeded to answer our next stupid question.

This is Wayne Gretzky as a player. Sometime in the eighties, during the Battle of Alberta (Edmonton vs. Calgary), 99 found himself with the puck at the side of the net, facing goaltender Mike Vernon. There was only a vertical toffee-box-sized opening between Vernon's pad and the goalpost. During his reign, innovation followed Gretzky around—redefining how to play behind the net, the stop and curl at the blueline, using the late man as a passing option, saucering the puck over his opponents' stick like none other—but in this instance, Wayne did something that you or I never would have. He flipped the puck on its side so that it stood straight up, then flung it at the net, configuring the rubber to match the gap in the goalie's armour. The story ends there. I'm not sure whether he scored or not, and, even though he totalled 1,016 goals, whether the puck went in the net is almost beside the point.

13 Parliament Hill
Shyam Selvadurai

In a country as large as ours, where national unity or even a sense of a nation is really a very ephemeral, insubstantial thing—a concept rather than a reality—the buildings of our federal government, and the surrounding gardens and landscape, stand as a much needed and valued concrete symbol of us as a country; they stand as the place from which that sense of country emanates. Hence, our great attachment to it and the value we ascribe to it even though the majority of Canadians have not visited Parliament Hill, and never will.

What I find interesting about the Parliament Buildings is that their very architecture defines who we are as a people. The choice of Gothic, rather than the neoclassical architecture of the U.S., was a very deliberate one. Gothic architecture was considered more democratic because its layout stressed serviceability and functionality over mere style. Its ornate carvings required the work of anonymous craftsmen who, while working within the bounds of an assigned framework and order, still had a lot of freedom to express their individuality. This idea of freedom within an ordered framework very much defines our values as a country.

Coming from Sri Lanka, where the legislature is secluded in the middle of a lake and barred to the general public, I was amazed at the openness of the grounds of Parliament Hill. It took me awhile to get used to having the freedom to walk around as I wished, to admire the flowers or eat my lunch on the lawn. I kept expecting someone to ask me my business and send me on my way. My favourite part of Parliament Hill is the Cat Sanctuary, tucked away among the trees behind the buildings, home since the 1970s to a community of stray cats, lovingly tended to by volunteers. Perhaps this, more than anything else, symbolizes our ideals of compassion and welcome.

14 Ottawa
J. L. Granatstein

The nation's capital has only two seasons, one of bone-chilling cold, the other of scorching humidity. A former lumber town, the city sits alongside the Ottawa River, with a pulp and paper mill on the Québec side rivalling the Parliament Buildings in splendour. Occupied by civil servants, all bilingual or struggling to become so to keep their jobs, the city has no culture, notwithstanding the presence of the National Arts Centre and the country's other national museums and monuments.

Such a description is wholly unfair but, Ottawa being what it is and Canada what it is, most Canadians do believe it to be so. Not as hated as Toronto, nor as cosmopolitan as Montréal or Vancouver, Ottawa in the spring, for example, is stunningly beautiful. The city is covered in tulips, and the Rideau Canal (in winter a long skating rink) cuts through the city's finest residential areas with wondrous views. The Library of Parliament, tucked in behind the Peace Tower, is the nation's architectural gem, and the new Canadian War Museum the country's only true historical museum.

But Ottawa is our political and administrative capital, the town where deputy ministers know that it is really they who are the permanent government, whatever Cabinet ministers might think. Ottawa is where politicians come to rule, with our grudging consent, and to spar, with much noise and feigned indignation. In truth, if the city has a bad reputation, it is because of its politicians and their constant attempts at scoring points rather than conducting the nation's business. To watch Question Period for more than two days is to despair of Canadian democracy and, unfortunately for the capital's standing, to detest the place where politicians work.

Queen Victoria, who made Ottawa the capital of the Province of Canada on the last day of 1857, would not have been amused.

15 Frederick Banting and the Discovery of Insulin
Christopher Moore

Insulin: it was the miracle cure of the 1920s. Until then, diabetics slowly wasted away as the very foods they ate poisoned their bodies, because they were unable to process sugars. Insulin injections gave them a near-instant reprieve from death.

Insulin's discovery also seemed miraculous. In 1921, twenty-nine-year-old Frederick Banting, an orthopedic surgeon with a hankering to discover something, got permission to spend the summer at the University of Toronto's research labs. Within a year, he was giving diabetics a new lease on life.

Scientists knew the pancreas was the key to the hormone called insulin. But no one had succeeded in extracting insulin. Banting theorized that if he sealed off the pancreas in live animals, it would atrophy without consuming its insulin-producing cells. That summer's experiments, undertaken with medical student Charles Best, proved his guess right. They quickly produced insulin from dog pancreases.

Next came a technical challenge. Producing reliable supplies of pure insulin confounded Banting and Best until two Toronto physiologists, J. J. MacLeod and J. P. Collip, joined the project. In January 1922, Banting had enough insulin to treat Leonard Thompson, a fourteen-year-old who was near death. Thompson made an immediate recovery (and lived until he was killed in a car accident in 1935).

Banting and Best made their patents freely available, and steady production of insulin made diabetes a treatable disease. Banting and MacLeod received the Nobel Prize in Medicine in 1923, and when Canada briefly returned to permitting Canadians to accept knighthoods in the 1930s, Banting became Sir Frederick Banting.

Banting, given a free hand to pursue further research, searched for more miracle cures, but without much success. He died in an airplane crash while assisting the war effort in 1941.

16 RCMP/Mounties
David Eddie

The RCMP evolved from the North-West Mounted Police (NWMP), created in 1873 by John A. Macdonald in response to the Cypress Hill Massacre, in which a combination of alcohol, a dispute over a missing horse, and tensions between whiskey traders, Métis, and wolf-hunters led to a shooting spree that left twenty-three Assiniboine men, women, and children dead.

The NWMP were charged with enforcing treaties with Canada's Native peoples, trying to control the burgeoning American whiskey trade in the area, and maintaining peace and order during the Klondike Gold Rush.

The force had mixed results in the first two departments, but it had spectacular success in the Klondike. The gold rush could have gone the other way: greed, gold, harsh conditions, an uncertain bureaucracy, prostitution, gambling—the Klondike was a tinderbox waiting to go kaboom.

But with Sam Steele—arguably the most famous Mountie of all time, celebrated in novels, TV shows, comic books, and even a computer game called "The Yukon Trail"—leading the way, the NWMP became legendary.

Thanks to Steele's iron-fist-in-velvet-riding-glove rule, along with inspired policies like the "ton of goods" rule (prospectors had to bring in at least a ton of goods with which to support themselves), the Klondike Gold Rush became the most peaceful and orderly such enterprise in history.

It made the image of a man astride a horse, in a red serge uniform and dimpled broad-brimmed hat, famous around the world and synonymous with Canada.

Canada's equestrian constabulary was anointed the Royal Canadian Mounted Police by King Edward VII in 1920. Since then, it has had many spectacular successes, made some mistakes, and had its share of tragedy (most notably, four officers shot and killed during a drug raid in Alberta in 2005).

But anywhere in the world, to this day, thanks in part to Sam Steele, when you say you're from Canada, people think of the Mountie who "always gets his man."

17 The CN Tower
Camilla Gibb

It was with great pride that I, as a child, boasted to my British grandparents that Toronto had the tallest free-standing structure in the world. Immigration to the colonies wasn't such a mistake, I sought to prove to them: we had the biggest, the brightest, the best of something, a telecommunications tower taller than either Russia's Ostankino or America's Sears Tower. We had a claim to world-class status in the form of this iconic, cloud-punching needle.

It's hard to imagine Toronto without the CN Tower. Although it stands above and somewhat apart from the city, it is by far the city's most defining architectural element. It made the Toronto skyline, gave it a focal point, a geographic heart. It's a point of orientation wherever you are in the city, and for many Torontonians, it has great sentimental value, at once a self-assured international statement and a reassuring sign of home.

Part of the tower's appeal is its Jetson-like design, an uncommonly bold display of 1970s modernism. The base is a hexagonal pillar, largely hollow, that houses the stairs, elevator shaft, plumbing, and wiring. A glass elevator facing the city whisks you up through the pillar at alarming speed, releasing you onto the main deck, at 346 metres, or the sky pod, 100 metres higher. The journey is an obligatory part of the tourist experience, as is staring through the glass floor of the observation deck hundreds of acrophobia-inducing metres straight down.

Beyond novelty and thrill, there is the glamour of the tower, perhaps best reflected in the revolving restaurant, which, in the spirit of the 1970s, was originally "Sparkles," the highest disco in the world.

We will ignore the irksome fact that we lost the claim to having the world's tallest free-standing structure to the Burj Dubai in 2007, because the CN Tower will always loom tallest of all towers in our hearts.

18 Old Québec City/Québec City
Roch Carrier

Old Québec City is a magical place. In a bookstore, flipping through pages, I find the name of one of my ancestors, an employee of the hospital in 1666. I cry out in surprise! And then, almost right afterwards, I come upon the name of his future wife, Barbe, whom he married in 1670. I am making a bit too much noise, and someone asks me, "Aren't you that writer?" We shake hands and he tells me his name: "Maheux." And once again I feel my senses leaving me, for I have just read the name Jean Maheu, merchant in Québec in 1666. This man, whom I met completely by chance, had an ancestor who had certainly known my own ancestor! At that time, Québec had a population of only 547 people!

Old Québec City has its ramparts, its narrow streets, its solid stone buildings that reflect an understated nobility. In this convent here, nuns and teachers knitted under-garments for the soldiers to keep them from freezing. In that hospital, people died in epidemics carried on the ships that came to port. In those houses, residents included explorers and travellers like Louis Jolliet, who explored the Mississippi; fur traders; *coureurs de bois*; soldiers who no longer wanted to do battle in Europe's wars and who stayed on in Old Québec City to become artisans and workers. In these other houses lived the colonial aristocracy and its governor, who enjoyed playing, dancing, drinking French wines, and dressing in the latest French fashions.

I have been to Québec City thousands of times, but when I arrive here, I still feel in my soul this special little warmth that no other city gives me.

Old Québec City tells us: "*Je me souviens.*"

19 Terry Fox
Camilla Gibb

In 1980, a twenty-one-year-old man with a prosthetic leg and bone cancer set himself a punishing challenge: to run the equivalent of a marathon every day for every kilometre between Canada's Atlantic and Pacific shores. His goal was simple: to raise one dollar for every Canadian, $24 million at the time, for cancer research.

I don't even need to tell you his name.

There is nothing that can be said about Terry Fox that hasn't been said before. He is one of our greatest heroes (second only to Tommy Douglas, according to votes cast for the CBC's "Greatest Canadian"), and his Marathon of Hope is, perhaps, the country's greatest inspirational sports story.

We watched his progress on the nightly news. Who can forget the image of a young man running at the side of a barren highway, his face strained, the little hiccup of his shoulders as he lifts that prosthetic leg, day after day under grey skies and, at first, to little applause. It's the loneliest picture in the world. One man who was doing it for all of us. One man who was all of us. Ordinary, his mother called him, and if that is so, then he challenges all of us, ordinary as we are, to do extraordinary things.

Terry Fox was halfway through his journey, close to Thunder Bay, when a doctor confirmed that the cancer had spread to his lungs. He gave that news to reporters himself. Lying on a stretcher, his voice trembling, he said that if he could get back out there and run again, he would. If there was any way. He died nine months later.

Before his death though, he surpassed that goal of $24 million. In the years since, his legacy, the Terry Fox Run, has raised more than $400 million. No individual has done more for cancer research in this country, nor drawn together so many people around the cause.

20 Confederation
Christopher Moore

1867. Got that? Eighteen sixty-seven. It is just about the only date you should always have handy to defend your Canadian History cred. July 1, 1867: the Confederation of Canada. To impress your friends, mention it was a Monday that year.

On July 1, 1867, Ontario, Québec, New Brunswick, and Nova Scotia became the founding provinces of the new Dominion of Canada. Even then, the plan of Confederation looked ahead to adding on the Canadian West, the North, Prince Edward Island, and Newfoundland. By 1880, the confederation covered all of Canada except Newfoundland, which became the tenth province of Canada in 1949.

The deal the founding provinces had struck was based on "federalism." Local things would be looked after locally, by the government of each province, and national matters would be handled by the new government of Canada, based in Ottawa. Just what was local and what was national? Well, Canadians would argue about that forever.

Canada in 1867 did not wish to remove itself from the British Empire, and Britain's monarch remained Canada's head of state. But the provinces already enjoyed "responsible government," which insured that the degree of independence they exercised would be up to them. Confederation in 1867, by uniting the separate colonies into a united federation, allowed the Canadian nation to control the pace of its own growth and development.

The British North America Act, which came into force on July 1, 1867, became Canada's Constitution. It has seen many small changes but only one large one: in 1982 it became "the Constitution Act," with a made-in-Canada amending formula and a new Charter of Rights and Freedoms.

Canadians have never ceased to argue about Confederation or to propose changes: the separation of one or more provinces, reforms to the Senate, changes to the monarchy. But the confederation negotiated in the 1860s has proven one of the world's most durable constitutions.

21 Alexander Graham Bell and the Invention of the Telephone
Ted Barris

Canada, the U.S., and Scotland all claim Alexander Graham Bell as their own. In fact, death nearly claimed him before any nation could.

Tuberculosis had already killed two of Alexander's brothers by 1870, when the Bell family moved from Boston to Brantford, Ontario. "I went to Canada to die," Alexander admitted later, but the southern Ontario climate proved an elixir.

At age twenty-six, Bell saw a French invention called the "phonotograph," which transferred sounds into patterns on the surface of smoked glass. Bell convinced a doctor friend to give him a dead man's ear bones so he could study the properties of sound. He noticed that it required very little power to register the human voice on his own crudely constructed phonotograph. Bell's discovery, together with drawings of his original "harmonic telegraph," sketched into his journal on July 2, 1874, depicted the world's first practical telephone.

The first successful demonstration occurred in March 1876, when Bell called his colleague, Thomas A. Watson, in the next room, saying, "Mr. Watson, come here! I want you." That summer, a soliloquy from *Hamlet* was recited over telephone lines between two buildings. A week later, Bell and his father exchanged greetings between Brantford and Paris, Ontario. Not only was this exchange history's first long-distance call, there was no charge.

From the moment of the telephone's creation, Canadians and Americans have argued over its official birthplace. In January 1876, Bell entrusted his patent application to a Canadian senator; the application was never registered. On March 7, 1876, the U.S. Patent Office registered Bell's "communication device." But even American claims to Bell's invention are murky; in 2002, the U.S. Congress conferred official recognition of the invention of the telephone to Antonio Meucci. As early as 1871, the Italian-born inventor had successfully built a communications link between the basement and first floor of his New York home, but had not patented it. Imagine TV ads inviting you to enroll in "Meucci Mobility."

22 World War I and World War II
J. L. Granatstein

The two great wars cost Canadians more than 100,000 dead and 226,000 wounded, a terrible price for a small country. In 1914, Canada had 8 million people and was a British colony that went to war automatically when the Mother Country did. A quarter-century later, 11 million Canadians had achieved formal independence, but once again went to war when Britain did, although the government waited one week to do so.

Both victorious wars spurred Canadian nationalism. English-speaking Canadians thrilled to the valour of their soldiers and saw the potential of their nation in the great deeds they accomplished. French-speaking Canadians, however, did not believe Canada was in any danger and furiously resented attacks on their reluctance to participate. The *nationalisme* that resulted was very different from that in the rest of Canada.

What all agreed on was that the two wars dramatically changed the country. Farmers could sell everything they grew, even as their children flooded into the cities to take well-paying jobs in war factories. Women took on every kind of work, and in World War II 50,000 women joined the armed forces. Parents and kids saved everything from cooking fats to milkweed pods, and the state borrowed vast sums from the people, with war bond campaigns becoming a feature of daily life. Total war involved everyone.

The economy boomed. In 1914, Canada had few manufacturing industries and during World War I produced mainly artillery shells. By the end of World War II, however, industry manufactured everything from bullets to bombers, turned out the vehicles that Allied armies rode to victory, and employed 1.2 million men and women.

Sadly, the government failed in World War I to provide real rewards for those who fought. It was not until after World War II that the Veterans Charter gave money, education, training, and land to those who had served. If wartime industrialization made modern Canada, so too did the veterans who came back.

23 Canadian Constitution/Charter of Rights and Freedoms/ Bill of Rights
Shyam Selvadurai

Our attachment to our newest Constitution of 1982 might come from our very gladness and relief that it exists at all. In a country where we citizens get along with remarkable amiability, it is often exasperating to witness the endless wrangling by federal and provincial powers and the continuous threats by Québec whenever any attempt at constitutional reform comes up. This squabbling is also worrying as it points to the fragility of our country. The Constitution, despite Québec's abstention, is a comforting sign of national unity; it tells us that we are a country.

A poll done in February 2002, on the twentieth anniversary of the Charter of Rights and Freedoms, found that 88 percent of Canadians felt the Charter was good for Canada. We have always believed ourselves to be more tolerant and humane than other nations, and this sense of our identity is now manifest in the Charter. The Charter has had a great impact on how I, as a gay man, live my life in this country. When I first came out in the 1980s, I was not protected under any law, and often felt at the mercy of employers and landlords. The public, politicians, and police were free to express their anti-gay rhetoric, and the sense that I was always a second-class citizen was an intolerable burden to live with. Now, the Charter has changed, for the better, the way I relate to my country and fellow citizens. That is the great gift of the Charter—it modulates, directs, and shapes the way we interact with each other, making us a decent, humane people and country. Whenever I think of how the Charter has changed us, a quote from Adrienne Clarkson always comes to mind: "Stumbling through darkness and racing through light, we have persisted in the creation of a Canadian civilization."

24 Diversity/Multiculturalism
Camilla Gibb

I grew up on an ordinary street in the middle of Toronto. Our neighbours were Italian and Chinese and Greek, and down the street I had a friend whose mother made pita bread every week, covering every available surface in plump, white, irresistible rounds. It all smelled too good, leading me to ask my friend where she came from. "Palestine," she said. I had to ask what Palestine was. "Well," she said, wisely, all of eight years old, "it's like a country."

We had moved from England a couple of years before, so I thought I knew what she meant—a country was a place you had left. An island where everybody looked and sounded like you and your name was ordinary, pronounceable.

Canada is not and will never be that. With the exception of the Aboriginal population, it is a country of people from elsewhere who have brought bits of their elsewheres with them. Some of these things we give up in order to live together as a nation. We agree on English and French as our common languages, we adhere to Canadian law, but we're also free to speak our native languages, practise our religions, and honour our cultural traditions.

Multiculturalism became government policy during the Trudeau era, setting the stage for constitutional recognition of multiculturalism as an official Canadian value in the Charter of Rights and Freedoms. It's an enlightened response to the diversity of our population; a policy governed by demographics. We wouldn't be viable as a nation, given our size, without immigration, hence we have one of the highest per capita rates of immigration in the world. Though multiculturalism is not without its problems and critics, it's hard not to celebrate the effort. We're engaged in a great experiment, unprecedented in the world. We are the world, or at least a noble attempt at conversation between all its peoples.

25 The Stanley Cup
David Eddie

It is the oldest professional sports trophy in North America: Lord Stanley of Preston bought the original cup from a London silversmith in 1892.

Since then, it's been growing. Every year, not only the players' names but also those of the managers, coaches, and club staff are inscribed on it. New rings are added every so often to accommodate all this verbiage, earning it the nickname "The Stovepipe Cup."

It's the only major sports trophy actually used as a cup, and every year players from the winning team drink champagne out of it.

But it's also been used as a toilet: in 1964, Toronto Maple Leaf Red Kelly posed for a photo with his infant son, only to discover later that his child had urinated in it. Years later, he said, he laughed every time he saw people drinking out of it.

It's been lost: in 1924, members of the Montréal Canadiens left it by the side of the road after changing a tire. (They found it later in the same spot.)

It's been stolen: in 1961, a Canadiens fan smashed a glass case in Chicago and ran off with it after the Habs lost the playoffs to the Black Hawks. "Your Honour," he told the judge, after being arrested, "I was simply bringing the Cup back to Montréal, where it belongs."

It's been thrown in a pool, to see if it floats (it doesn't). It's been drop-kicked, burned, dented, and repaired numerous times, once in an auto shop.

The engraving is riddled with mistakes. Dickie Moore's name is spelled five different ways on the Cup; Jacques Plante's name four different ways.

But somehow all these battle scars, all this history, only add to its lustre. Is it the best trophy to win in all of professional sports? Certainly it is the dream of every hockey player to skate around the rink, holding it aloft in front of a cheering crowd.

26 The Calgary Stampede
Todd Babiak

Flying into Calgary, nothing immediately "western" announces itself. The taxi ride into the city's tidy downtown weaves between soft industrial areas, strip malls, and some of the most impressive urban sprawl in North America. Yet for ten days every July, during the Stampede, Calgary becomes a boisterous cowboy town. Oil executives and bankers dress in boots and hats and handkerchiefs.

The hills and grasslands of southern Alberta are dotted with ranches, and have been since the late nineteenth century. So it seemed natural when, in 1912, four wealthy Calgarians decided to inaugurate a monstrous Wild West show. With an impressive purse, the first Calgary Stampede attracted huge crowds and rodeo talent from across the continent.

Today, the rodeo portion of the Stampede is in the background. These days, it's a dress-up party and an opportunity to celebrate, with beer and pancake breakfasts, an essential piece of Alberta's personal mythology: maverick-hood.

There is a debate within Calgary about the city's cowboy brand. Some worry that the Stampede is a Canadian take on an American notion, silly and conservative, unbefitting a city that increasingly considers itself cosmopolitan and progressive. The chuckwagon race portion of the rodeo is particularly controversial, as horses are often injured or killed. Yet outside the borders of the university and certain central neighbourhoods, the Stampede enjoys enormous support among Calgarians.

To consolidate thematically and physically, during a time of unprecedented expansion and change in Calgary, the non-profit Stampede Society is transforming the exhibition grounds into a year-long attraction. They plan to build a casino and an "olde tyme" main street market area.

The Stampede's tagline is "The Greatest Outdoor Show on Earth." At least a million people visit the exhibition grounds southeast of downtown Calgary over the course of a twenty-first-century Stampede. They consume over 75,000 hamburgers.

27 Céline Dion
Roch Carrier

Everybody loves a fairy tale, for example the one about a poor little girl, with twelve sisters and brothers, who becomes a rich and beautiful princess...

In the morning paper one day in 1981, what was the great news of the day? I can't remember. But I do remember a minor item: after listening to a demo tape from a young unknown singer, a music promoter had decided to remortgage his house to support her career, because he believed that this girl, Céline, would be listened to all over the world.

In 1984, the talented adolescent sang for the Pope and 65,000 spectators at Montréal's Olympic Stadium. It was just the beginning.

Ten years later, Céline Dion married that same intrepid promoter, who had been right about her future all along.

In fairy tales, fate is dictated by magic. Céline's fate is different. In her story, the magic is her will to succeed, her consistency, and her persistence.

Nobody can fully understand her everyday life: her need to express in her shows and recordings a sound that touches souls; her obligation to please, even on days when she doesn't feel like it, to smile, when all she wants to do is cry; the difficulty of conforming to the image people create of her; the endless submission to a strategic plan and a demanding schedule. Every day, she has to climb one step higher on the ladder of fame. She has to find a way to last in a universe where memories fade in days.

People love this princess, who lives in castles but who admits that her most cherished dream is to have a clothesline in her garden, just like the one in her mother's garden in sub-urban Montréal.

So many little girls are inspired by Céline Dion's incredible success to dream and to build their dreams in Canada, where anything is possible.

28 Canadian National Railways
J. L. Granatstein

World War I stretched Canada's railways to the utmost, so much so that all of the over-extended large lines, except for Canadian Pacific, went into or faced imminent bankruptcy. The government of Sir Robert Borden could not permit this in wartime, and after a royal commission, moved to nationalize the Canadian Northern in 1917 and the Grand Trunk and Grand Trunk Pacific Railroads in 1919. A subsidiary effect—preservation of some of the shareholders' wealth and Canada's reputation as a good investment—was also largely achieved, though there were many complaints, not least from British investors.

Incorporated in 1919, the Canadian National Railways (CNR) name came into effect in 1923, and under the effective leadership of Sir Henry Thornton, the CNR expanded into radio (the CN Tower is a later product of this interest in telecommunications), ships and ferries, hotels, and resource industries, and even laid the foundations of Trans-Canada Airlines. To travel across Canada on the CNR's fine passenger trains meant travelling (and dining) in style.

Inevitably, however, spiralling costs caught up with a railway funded by the government and therefore prey to political pressure. Passenger traffic became uneconomical and by the 1980s was moved to Via Rail. Then the constraints of being a Crown corporation responsible to the government became too onerous, and the CN was privatized in 1995. This, in addition to deregulation the following year, permitted the closure of little-used lines and other cost-cutting measures. As the North American Free Trade Agreement came into effect in the 1990s, CN found itself well placed to take advantage, and it did so with shrewd acquisitions of U.S. rail lines. Now profitable and operating more than 50,000 kilometres of track in the U.S. alone, CN is a success story: the trains, carrying every kind of freight, run on time.

29 Toronto
David Eddie

Everyone all across the country seems to love to hate it.

But why? It's a beautiful city: it has so many trees and forests it almost looks like a forest from the air. It's been called "Toronto the Good," "the world's most liveable city," a "city of neighbourhoods," and "the world's most multicultural city."

Architecturally, it's unpretentious, a ragtag mishmash of styles. Ethnically, it's a manic mosaic, dotted with Little Italies, Little Portugals, Little Koreas, Little Everything. Those who need to get away can go to Toronto Island, where you can have a picnic, rent a bike, or (for those who really need to get away) hop on a plane and take off.

It's one of the world's top ten economic engines. Yet it consistently rates in the top twenty, and sometimes at the number one spot, in comparisons of which cities are the most pleasant to live in.

And most Torontonians seem to know it, too. A recent poll reported that four out of five Torontonians rated their quality of living as either "good" or "very good."

And that's precisely what seems to annoy non-Torontonian Canadians: "Oooh, Torontonians are so smug." But it's a fundamental misreading of the city's character, I think.

Imagine if Toronto were a person. "I've got the world's biggest (bookstore)! The tallest (CN Tower, regrettably just passed by some monstrosity that will probably fall over in Dubai)! The longest (road: Yonge St.)!"

You'd want to say: "Hey, take it easy, buddy. You don't have to impress me. I already thought you were pretty great anyway."

Shyness often looks like snobbery at first glance, and we all know that the insecure boast the most. Whenever a dignitary of any stature visits this pleasant little burg, they're always asked the same thing: "What do you think of *us*?"

Toronto underestimates its worth and is haunted by self-doubt. Which is exactly what makes it the quintessential Canadian city.

Vimy

France
1917

30 Vimy Ridge
J. L. Granatstein

The most famous Canadian victory of World War I, the capture of the great ridge in northern France by the Canadian Corps, has been celebrated ever since. Although it deserves commemoration, it was not hugely significant in military terms. Yes, the Germans entrenched on Vimy Ridge had beaten off earlier French and British assaults; yes, the Canadians, all four divisions fighting together for the first time, succeeded. But the battle changed nothing. The Germans retreated a few kilometres, and the bloody war went on exactly as before for another nineteen months.

So why the Vimy legend? Because the Canadian Corps had become very good, and its British commander, General Julian Byng, knew how to lead, and picked the best officers as his subordinates. The nationalist Canadian public (but not the soldiers) soon forgot that they had been led by Byng, and most assume that General Arthur Currie, then First Division commander, led the assault. He didn't, although his role in planning was important in the victory.

The public at home also assumed that their soldiers had scaled a great cliff, struggling to climb to the top. In fact, the ridge facing the Canadians had only a gradual rise, with the steep drop behind the German lines.

Nor was Vimy a bloodless victory. Canadian casualties in the assault numbered almost 11,000, relatively cheap in Great War terms, but hardly bloodless. No, Vimy was hailed because the Allies had had few successes up to that time and needed a triumph to celebrate.

So what really happened on that Easter of 1917? Vimy Ridge was a carefully planned set piece attack that mustered huge quantities of supplies and vast arrays of artillery, aircraft, engineers, and signallers to support four infantry divisions in a straight-ahead assault. What was most significant was that the confident Canadian Corps learned that day that it could fight and win.

31 Plains of Abraham
Ted Barris

Canadians might refer to the events of this place as "Canada's 15 minutes of fame." Though the military engagement on the Plains of Abraham occurred half a world from the chief combatants of the Seven Years War—Britain and France—the short, sharp battle near the fortress of Québec in New France on September 13, 1759, determined the future of Canada.

Attempting to defend 200 years of French colonial investment in North America, Lieutenant-General the Marquis de Montcalm arranged his 5,000 troops in what his opponent, British Major-General James Wolfe called "inaccessible entrenchments" around the citadel of Québec. Unable to dislodge the French with artillery and facing the prospect of a winter stalemate, Wolfe had to either abandon the siege or strike unexpectedly with his 5,000 troops. He chose the latter at a small cove on the St. Lawrence, from which a path led right up a cliff to the Plains of Abraham.

In the darkness of a moonlit night and what British Rear-Admiral Charles Holmes described as "the most profound silence," Wolfe dispatched a detachment of troops in small boats. The 1,800 British regulars scaled the 50-metre cliffs and overran Montcalm's position. By daylight, Wolfe had his entire force ashore and marched onto the Plains of Abraham.

"There they are, where they have no right to be," Montcalm exclaimed. He had no choice but to attack before the British consolidated. Wolfe drew up his regulars into a long line, two men deep. Montcalm's militia launched an assault six men deep. The British held their fire until the French were within 36 metres. Wolfe's thin red line held, and shattered the French advance. Montcalm, attempting to rally his forces, and Wolfe, pushing for victory, were both killed.

A quarter-hour after it began, the battle on the Plains of Abraham was history. The resulting Treaty of Paris (1763) confirmed British control of New France. The subsequent Act of Québec, in 1774, allowed the colony to keep its language and religion.

John A. Macdonald
Christopher Moore

"**T**here are wheels in that man which have never been turned yet," said a cabinet minister who had worked with him for years and still found him a mystery.

Everyone knows he drank and joked and procrastinated. We've heard about the scandals. He was probably not easy to be married to. He's been dead and gone more than a hundred years. Yet John A. Macdonald's standing and reputation continue to rise.

Not just the bronze-statue kind of reputation—the father of the country, the first prime minister, the man who built the railroad. As we see leaders and prime ministers strive and struggle and exit the stage, observers of Canadian politics gain ever more respect for the sheer skill with which Macdonald led the country for most of the period from 1856 until his death.

John A. Macdonald (1815–1891) was Scots by birth. He grew up near Kingston, Ontario, and was first elected to the colonial legislature in 1844. He soon proved himself a master of parliamentary techniques and a genius in judging, persuading, motivating—and sometimes manipulating—his fellow politicians and the public. Cautious and conservative in philosophy, he was called "Old Tomorrow" for his willingness to wait for the right moment. Still, he could be ruthless and bold too, gambling his political future time and again on his alliance with Georges-Étienne Cartier of Québec, on the success of the national railway, or in deciding that Louis Riel would hang despite all the calls for clemency.

Already a government leader in pre-Confederation Canada, Macdonald was at first skeptical about the plan for Confederation. But his organizing skills gradually made him the key figure in achieving Confederation, and he became Canada's first prime minister. Defeated by scandal in 1873, he roared back to power in 1878. He was still prime minister when he died in 1891.

"Canada is a hard country to govern," he once said. John A. proved up to the challenge.

33 David Suzuki
Michelle Berry

David Suzuki has spent his entire life taking complicated scientific theories and facts and making them interesting and understandable. That's quite a feat. Remember him on *The Nature of Things*, his hair all poofy, his eyes wild, hands moving excitedly? It might have been that crazy hair (now tamed), but he was, and still is, mesmerizing. His voice is especially memorable. The issues he discusses are vast and varied: space, wilderness, environment, sustainable energy, to name a few.

David Suzuki was born in 1936 in Vancouver. The Suzuki family was interned during the war. The government of Canada sold Suzuki's father's dry cleaning business and sent him to a labour camp, yet David Suzuki remains a dedicated and proud Canadian.

Originally educated in the U.S. as a geneticist, Suzuki began to concentrate on the environment before it was popular to do so. Many of his first predictions—on global warming, on clean energy and the environment, on our human footprint--have come true. He was often taken to task by more "pure" scientists who felt Suzuki had sold out to popular science. In 2004, David Suzuki was ranked fifth in the CBC's "The Greatest Canadian," after Tommy Douglas (Suzuki's own choice), Terry Fox, Pierre Elliott Trudeau, and Sir Frederick Banting. Yes, that makes him popular, but look at the impressive company he's listed with. That's a good kind of popularity.

Suzuki can be controversial (once asking McGill University students to see if there was a legal way to put some of our leaders in jail, for example), but that's one of the best ways to get his message across. The David Suzuki Foundation works hard on our behalf to "find ways for society to live in balance with the natural world that sustains us." Attending rallies, speaking to governments, raising a little hell here and there, has served him, and us, well.

34 Montréal
Dave Bidini

First, an apology. While I know that Montréal rests at Canada's political crossroads and has been forever close to the heartbeat of our nation's art and history, this thumbnail is largely about love. Montréal's cultural tolerance, open streets, and freedom of spirit make it singular within a nation that's only now starting to become liberated from itself. One can travel to western Newfoundland, Nunavut, and the B.C. coast and find true exoticism within our borders, but Montréal and perhaps Québec City are the only two interior cities where you feel as if you're outside of Canada while still in it.

In 1988, I was working at the CBC as a replacement host for the music program *Brave New Waves*. At the time, my girlfriend was studying at Concordia, and had an apartment on Clark Street, just off the Main, with a front and back balcony view of the streets. During our time there, we did lots of nothing, which was unusual coming from a city—Toronto—that insisted its citizens always be doing something. It was a great summer: the Expos were not only alive, but competitive; rent was outrageously cheap; and the post-referendum blues had caused an exodus of businesses, leaving communities filled with artists, who never need much money to live. The streets took us in and we fell in love.

Last year, I competed in an adult hockey tournament in the city's Mont Royal neighbourhood. The rink was on a boulevard of cafés, bakeries, and taverns. One morning before a game, I secured a caffe latte from a nearby Franco-Italian café and stared out the window as snow fell lightly through the cold sunshine. Outside, a handful of skiers skidded along frozen sidewalks, while behind them a chugging snow blower parked atop a huge snowbank. The driver entered the café and removed her helmet to reveal a long smile, a sleek mane of black hair, and dancing eyes, exuding the kind of cool beauty that only this city could have produced.

35 Wilderness
Tomson Highway

I have had the privilege of circumnavigating the globe three times and have been to fifty-three countries. I have, therefore, seen many wonders, from the fjords of Norway to the glaciers of Greenland, the deserts of Morocco, the Great Barrier Reef, the Amazon jungle, and so on, and it is a perfect thrill to see these places. But each time I arrive back in Canada, I never cease to be amazed at the natural wonders that make up my country, from the craggy cliffs of Cape Spear in eastern Newfoundland to the fishing villages of Nova Scotia, the Saguenay River in Québec, the French River system in northern Ontario, the 10,000 lakes (I kid you not) of subarctic Manitoba, the prairies of Saskatchewan, the coulees of southern Alberta, the Rockies, the Queen Charlotte Islands, the northern lights of Dawson City, Yukon, the endless barrens of the Northwest Territories, the icebergs of Nunavut, awesome, awesome sights every one of them. And it's not just the beauty of them all, it is the endless variety. There is no other country like it in the world.

I was born in the heart of it (in northern Manitoba); I live in the heart of it (in northern Ontario) and will for the rest of my life. At this lakeside cottage where I live summers, just for instance, between beautiful Lake Nipissing and Georgian Bay, I am surrounded by wildlife: the robins who make their nest under our deck every spring, right outside our front door, the pair of painted turtles in the lake—Pilar and Juan Antonio, we call them—who walk across the lawn to our house on a basis semi-regular, James the chipmunk, who lives in a hole under my office, the crane, the hawk, Sam the garter snake, Harry the hare, the deer, the finches—we are surrounded.

The forest sings, the forest is alive: Canada's wilderness—our wilderness—has a soul!

36 Tommy Douglas
David Eddie

He was a fighter.

At the age of eighteen, weighing 61 kilograms, he competed in a wrestling match for the Lightweight Championship of Manitoba. It was a six-round match, during which he lost several teeth and strained his hand and thumb. He won.

As a young child he injured his leg and developed osteomyelitis, a wasting infection of the bone marrow. The leg would have been amputated if it had not been for a doctor who thought the case would be a good subject to teach his students, and treated Tommy for free.

The incident left an impression on young Tommy. He became determined that no one should have to rely on the whims of human generosity for free health care.

Many years later, in his first term in office as premier of Saskatchewan, after leading the CCF party to victory in 1944 and creating the first democratic socialist government in North America, he launched the first salvo in a lifelong battle for universal free medicine.

It would be a long fight. Douglas's successor as premier of Saskatchewan, Woodrow Lloyd, finally launched Saskatchewan's public health program in 1962. In 1966, the minority government of Lester B. Pearson created a federal universal health care program, with the feds and the provinces each paying half.

Douglas was also the first head of any government of Canada to call for a constitutional bill of rights.

Ironically, none of this might have happened if not for that childhood leg injury. At the outbreak of World War II, Douglas enlisted in the Canadian Army, but a medical examination identified his leg problems. While Douglas stayed in Canada, his regiment, the Winnipeg Grenadiers, headed for Hong Kong, where most of them were killed or captured in 1941.

Douglas was spared, and went on to accomplish all the great things that led him to be voted the greatest Canadian, ever, in the CBC's 2004 competition.

37 The Loonie
Michelle Berry

At the top of the Wikipedia link to the loonie it says, "This article is about the coin. For the Canadian dollar as a currency, see 'Canadian dollar.' For a mentally ill person, see 'lunatic.'" Is it just me or do you also find this funny? The U.S. has their greenback and we have our loonie—easily confused with *One Flew Over the Cuckoo's Nest*. Only in Canada.

I remember when the loonie came out. I remember groaning, pocket/purse full of heavy coins. I remember thinking that the coin somehow devalued the dollar, that mixing it up with measly pennies and nickels made it somehow worth less. But then I got used to it. Quickly. You give a loonie to the guy on the street, or a toonie, which appeared in 1996, to your kid to take to school for pizza lunch. There is a jar with quite a few coins on my kitchen counter. They are pretty, bronze-plated, large. A loon. A copper polar bear surrounded by a nickel ring. Now I can't even remember the look of those flimsy paper bills. Traditions have been made with loonies—lucky ones are buried in ice during significant hockey games, tooth fairies leave loonies under pillows, and allowances are paid in coin.

The original concept for the loonie was a picture of a voyageur, but, in 1987, the sample coin was lost en route to the Royal Canadian Mint in Winnipeg and the design had to be changed to stop any counterfeiting. A voyageur. Now that would have been interesting. Imagine: "Do you have change for a voyageur?" or "Can you spare a voyageur?"

The loonie definitely buys less than that one-dollar bill did in 1987. I was right. But that has everything to do with inflation and nothing to do with its jangling weight in our pockets.

38 Freedom
Shyam Selvadurai

Freedom is an ambiguous word, since what we each consider freedom is often different and conflicting. Its inclusion on the list could mean many things. On the one hand, perhaps Canadians feel that we ought to celebrate our impressive record here and abroad as champions of freedom; we ought to cherish the fact that we enjoy an exceptional amount of freedom compared with most other nations. In many international rankings, Canada ranks as one of the top countries to live in, based on the quality of life and freedom its citizens enjoy.

On the other hand, Canada, like all nations of the world, does have a history of denying or suppressing freedom. There is the interning of Japanese-Canadians, the Chinese head tax, the immigration policies that effectively barred non-whites from entering this country until the 1960s, the horrendous abuse and destruction of Aboriginal people—all this during a time when Canadians considered themselves the very paragons of freedom and civilized society. In the name of bringing "freedom," Canada has also come under criticism for its military role in the war on Afghanistan.

Then there is the troubling issue of domestic security—how to balance freedom with the vigilance needed to fend off a terrorist attack. Perhaps those of us who come from countries where we have seen the way people behave when they feel threatened, seen the way a country, in the face of terrorism, can slide so quickly from democracy and freedom to a virtual police state, are concerned with the dilemma of how to protect national security without unnecessarily eroding the liberty we cherish. Perhaps we know the true value of the freedom we enjoy here, even more than those who have never been deprived of it. Perhaps we voted freedom onto the list so our nation can guard and protect it.

38 Québec
Christopher Moore

Pas comme les autres, a province not like the others: that is the first thing to remember about the province of Québec. Québec has always had a unique role as the heartland, shield, and advocate for francophone language and culture in Canada.

At first, "Québec" was a First Nations place name, then the name of the French colonial town. During the French regime, the area around Québec City was called "Canada" or "New France." It was the British who first named the colony "Québec," and then renamed it "Lower Canada."

The Province of Québec came into being at Confederation, in 1867. Québecers asserted the right to "our language, our laws, and our institutions," and the province has always claimed a unique role in ensuring that French language and culture survives and thrives in North America.

At first, Québecers entrusted their *survivance* more to their Catholic faith and a traditional rural way of life than to the government of Québec. In the mid-twentieth century, as Québecers embraced modern, secular, and urban ways of living, the state's role grew more important, and the provincial government of Québec asserted its authority as the principal representative of Québecers. As Québec and Canada clashed over the boundaries of federal and provincial authority, many Québecers came to support sovereignty for Québec.

In 2006, the federal government officially recognized the Québécois as a nation within a united Canada. Québec's provincial legislature is called the Assemblée Nationale, the national assembly of Québec.

Today, immigration is making Québec an increasingly multi-ethnic society, but 80 percent of the province's 7.5 million people still count French as their mother tongue. Québec has flourished as the centre of French in North America for 400 years, and it will continue to do so far into the future.

40 Maple Syrup
Dave Bidini

If anyone ever criticizes Canada for being a young country, tell them that you drink sap and leave it at that. Drinking sap makes us sound ancient, wise, industrious. The evolution of drinking sap--which is to say, maple syrup—came when a group of people who lived a long time ago (possibly the Algonquins) discovered (possibly before recorded history) that eating sap was good for you. Natives would tomahawk V-shaped incisions into bark, drawing the gooey liquid into buckets. These buckets would be left outside so that a layer of ice would form over the sap, turning it into concentrate. This effect could also be achieved by boiling the sap, but that came later. History, in fact, gets muddy when trying to figure out the hows and whys of making maple syrup, but, through all of this, one thing is certain: we like to drink sap.

The process of making maple syrup is also a rite of passage, for almost every young Canadian east of the Prairies has visited a maple syrup (or maple sugar) farm on a field trip as a child. The maple syrup field trip is one of the few reprieves one gets from school in the wintertime; that and skating for an afternoon at the local rink. To me, eating maple syrup means riding a clunky bus, wearing my parka, as my classmates and I headed through the city to a snowbound field with a few wooden buildings and a forest of birch trees with spikes nailed into them. It means red cheeks and hot sugar, cold toes and snowball fights, and my parents hugging me desperately after a long day away. While the taste of maple syrup is the taste of history and the land—and the culinary link between us and our fore-bears—to me, the taste of maple syrup is also the taste of adventure. It's like being home and away in a single spoonful.

41 Moose
David Eddie

You do not want to hit one with your car.

Because of their height and weight—a bull can weigh as much as 800 kilograms (1,500 pounds) and stand 2 metres tall—when struck by a car, a moose will often come crashing down on the windshield and roof of the car, crushing and either killing or seriously injuring the occupants. In New Brunswick alone, there are over 300 moose–motor-vehicle collisions every year. At the very least, your car will be totalled. And quite often, the moose will survive.

The moose is the national animal of both Sweden and Norway, and the state animal of Maine. Here in Canada, though, it lost out to the beaver, an animal that perhaps better captures our gnawing ambition and self-doubt, and busybody, workaholic tendencies.

But moose are plentiful in this country: Canada's moose population is estimated at between 500,000 and 1 million head. Which is amazing for such a big, hungry beast. They move around a lot in search of food, and because of their stature can travel far.

Moose, though monstrous (the largest member of the deer family), are vegetarian. During the summer, they eat as much as 11 to 14 kilograms of "forage" per day, but, unlike bears, they are not interested in the drumsticks or ham sandwiches in your picnic basket.

They are largely peaceful. But they have been known to attack. In spring, cows (moose moms) may have young calves about, and here's a little common-sense backwoods survival tip: don't come between a cow and her calf.

Most dangerous though is the fall: mating season. A bull moose may perceive you as a threat or even a rival for a cow's affections, and may not act with full rationality. Bull moose in full courtship mode have even been known to charge passing trains.

Mainly though, like most sensible animals, they try to stay away from humans as much as possible.

42 Wildlife
Michelle Berry

In Freiburg, Germany, taped to a travel agency's front window, there is a poster advertising Canada, with snow-peaked Rocky Mountains in the distance; in the foreground, just behind the big letters KANADA, is a family of grizzly bears stepping lightly into a river, looking for salmon.

Whales (humpback, killer, right), bears (brown, black, polar), salmon (chinook, coho, pink), sea lions, seals, moose, beavers, loons, and, of course, the always unpopular mosquitoes and Canada geese. From the West Coast to the East Coast, from way up north to our major cities, Canada is brimming with wildlife. What, besides the forests and oceans, shouts "Canada" more than the animals and sea life? Do you see moose in Florida? (Maybe at Disneyworld) What about beavers? Like the koala bear in Australia, the beaver is a pest, but it's *our* pest. The little furry, tree-destroying, buck-toothed terror is, after all, on our nickel. Look at our money: animals everywhere. The loonie, the quarter (moose head), and the toonie (a polar bear).

If we are dwarfed by the vastness of our environment, then we are made stronger by the wildlife within it. By monitoring and watching our wildlife, we can see the differences humans are making (for better or worse). In Toronto's overpopulated Beaches area, the raccoons are taking over. Strangely, after a very cold, snowy winter, a bear was tranquillized and relocated after it roamed through the backyards of Pickering, Ontario. Animals, like the canary in the coal mine, warn us of danger.

Canadian wildlife defines who we are not only to others in the world, but to ourselves. I know we all want to get rid of the Canada goose (have you ever tried to picnic on Toronto Island?), but when I saw them in Florida recently (at Disneyworld, actually), our messy, huge snowbirds, I thought, hey, there's a little piece of Canada—and it's pestering others.

43 Stephen Harper
Todd Babiak

It is helpful to consider Canada's 22nd prime minister in relation to the man whose policies arguably influenced him most: Pierre Trudeau.

Like Canada's most iconic prime minister, Harper was an intellectual before he entered politics. Like Trudeau, who was a Roman Catholic, Harper is a religious man.

Harper became serious about politics thanks to Trudeau's National Energy Program (NEP), which radicalized a generation of young Albertans and has passed into the realm of conservative mythology.

Unlike Trudeau, Prime Minister Stephen Harper has always been a member of the middle class, an average Canadian. This has inspired commentators, who apparently prefer Starbucks, to refer to his supporters as "Tim Hortons Conservatives."

Harper grew up in Toronto, where he was a member of the Young Liberals. He left U of T after two months, to finish his studies in Edmonton, then Calgary. His political sympathies did not move with him; by the mid-1980s, Harper was a Young Progressive Conservative.

After a series of shocks and disillusionments, Harper moved from the PCs to the nascent Reform Party—led by Preston Manning, who would become a mentor and, eventually, a rival. After a stint in the House of Commons as a Reform MP, Harper led the National Citizens Coalition, and eventually returned to the House of Commons as a Canadian Alliance MP for Calgary Southwest and Leader of the Official Opposition.

Harper helped unite the right and create the Conservative Party of Canada. He became leader in 2004, and the new party defeated the Liberals, led by Paul Martin, in January 2006.

As prime minister, leading a minority government, Harper has been a staunch supporter of free trade and tax cuts, the war in Afghanistan, improved relations with the United States, northern sovereignty and a new—and yet to be fully defined—accommodation between Québec and the rest of Canada.

44 Lester B. Pearson
J. L. Granatstein

Mike Pearson—the nickname was given him by his Great War flying instructor because Lester sounded too prissy—was the beau ideal for Canadians in the 1950s. He had served in World War I, taught university, joined the country's tiny Department of External Affairs, and during World War II played a major role in creating a stronger Canada in a free world. Then he went into politics, helped write the North Atlantic Treaty, and invented the idea of United Nations peacekeeping during the Suez Crisis of 1956. The Nobel Peace Prize he won for his herculean efforts in New York seemed to be the cap on his career, one that inspired young Canadians then, and still.

Pearson's career still had steam in it, however. In 1957, the Liberal Party, then in Opposition, chose Mike as leader, and for the next six years he fought against John Diefenbaker's inept, bumbling Conservative government. Despite his trademark lisp, his bad French, and his awkward television manner, Pearson nonetheless won over the electorate. In 1963, he took power.

Over the next five years, Pearson's government created an astonishing legislative record, with the Canada Pension Plan, the Auto Pact, the groundwork for medicare, the Royal Commission on Bilingualism and Biculturalism, a new flag, and the unification of the armed forces. Pearson stumbled repeatedly, his scandal-prone Cabinet leaked like a sieve, and his ministers continuously and openly jockeyed for succession. But somehow Mike Pearson kept the country afloat during troubled times with the Americans, who were engaged in the Vietnam War; Québec's Quiet Revolution; and the Cold War.

Cartoonist Duncan Macpherson captured Pearson beautifully when he showed him as a bespectacled baseball player hit on the head by a fly, then bobbling the ball, only to snag it just before it hit the ground. "The Old Smoothie," the great cartoonist called him. Exactly right.

45 The Grey Cup
Todd Babiak

In 1909, Birks Jewellers built a handsome trophy for Earl Grey, then Governor General of Canada. It became Canada's professional football trophy and, in the middle years of the twentieth century, operated as an instrument of Canadian unity—bringing together east and west, and French and English. The cup itself is a fragile artifact. The Edmonton Eskimos alone have broken the trophy three times, by dropping it, sitting on it, and, most recently, head-butting it.

Since 1948, when the Calgary Stampeders expanded the Canadian Football League championship event into a week-long series of festivities, the Grey Cup has been a November festival as much as a game.

Today, the Grey Cup is the most-watched sporting event on TV in Canada. Grey Cup parties are common in living rooms across the country, accompanied by salty snacks and beer. Yet as Canada's cities grow, and as the cultural mix of the country becomes more complex, it's difficult to imagine the Grey Cup as an event that brings the country together. The Grey Cup brings together Canadians who like salty snacks, beer, and football.

In the 1990s, half-time performers were traditional rock and roll artists like Trooper, the Nylons, and Tom Cochrane. The Guess Who serenaded the Grey Cup into the twenty-first century, solidifying the blue-collar, baby-boomer sensibility of the event.

In recent years, organizers and broadcasters have attempted to broaden the appeal of the Grey Cup for younger viewers; recent half-time performers have included Lenny Kravitz, Nelly Furtado, and American hip-hop-and-pop outfit, Black Eyed Peas.

In 2006, the CFL announced that corporate naming rights were available for the Grey Cup championship—if not the trophy itself. Sports radio call-in shows lit up with objections that the game, a Canadian institution and one of the country's few sacred spaces, should not be for sale.

The league has entertained offers, but the Grey Cup remains unbranded.

46 The Olympics
Shyam Selvadurai

The Olympics is a puzzling addition to the list, given that it is not specifically a Canadian thing, given that we have hosted only two Olympics so far, and given that the games come around only every four years. Further, given recent instances of bribery, corruption, and doping, plus the massive costs to the host country—which effectively prevents the games from ever being hosted by a developing nation—and its domination by giant corporations, the Olympics seems rather out of step with our Canadian values of smallness and fairness and quiet patriotism. So what does this inclusion say about us? Perhaps countries, like people, can be paradoxical: even while we esteem the above values, we find massive displays of ostentation and nationalism appealing. But then, perhaps it is on the list because so many Canadians love sports and give so much of their time to it. When we watch our athletes perform, we experience the thrill of transference—that imaginative melding of our lesser abilities to their greater ones, so that we too fly effortlessly over hurdles, skim the surface of pools at lightning speed, score those winning goals.

On the other hand, perhaps the Olympics is on the list because we are concerned that, given its dismal human rights record, China was selected as a host country for the 2008 Olympics. Perhaps we are concerned that Canada's participation in the Olympics shows, if not explicit support for the repressive regime in China, at least our decision to stay uncritical. Then again, given the massive financial burden of the Olympics, perhaps respondents included the games in the list because they want careful attention paid to the price of hosting the Olympics in Vancouver. They want us to debate the way we will host the games—a way that must show the world the values we stand for as a nation.

47 Expo 67
J. L. Granatstein

"The greatest thing we have ever done as a nation," or so journalist Peter C. Newman described Expo 67, the "Universal and International Exhibition" staged in Montréal to mark Canada's Centennial. It may even have been true.

Certainly the cost was enormous—$283 million, when a million dollars was still a large sum. The attendance was amazing, with 50 million paid admissions over the six months Expo 67 was open, double the original estimates. And Montréal, still the greatest city in Canada, looked spectacular, a booming bicultural city full of life, music, well-dressed people, and spectacular buildings in town and especially on the Expo site.

That site, created on Île Ste. Hélène and the newly created Île Notre Dame in the St. Lawrence River, featured stunning national pavilions. The Soviet Union's was a soaring modern structure showing Soviet achievements in space and the predictable bust of Lenin. The United States' pavilion, a twenty-storey-high geodesic dome designed by the visionary Buckminster Fuller, glowed brilliantly at night and shone in the sun. Some 120 governments and hundreds of private exhibitors had pavilions or displays, many showcasing national treasures and featuring state-of-the-art multiscreen media. It was a smash hit, an incredible celebration of Canada's hundred years, all done to the tune of Bobby Gimby's catchy "Ca-na-da" theme.

Or was it? Most of Expo's buildings came down as planned at the end of the great fair. Montreal's great reputation for joie de vivre began to fade quickly as separatism, sparked by French President Charles de Gaulle's 1967 visit to Quebec and his *"Vive le Québec libre"* speech, soon resulted in an exodus of anglophones and corporate head offices. Canada entered a period of existential crisis that would last for at least the next thirty years. Expo 67 was a triumph, yes, but, inevitably, a transitory one.

48 Bilingualism
Roch Carrier

French-English bilingualism is the cornerstone of this complex, imposing construction we call Canada.

In my village in Québec, close to the American border, Monsieur Rancourt was the only person who could speak English as well as French. He had learned it in the army, during World War I, but was gradually forgetting it. When an American fisherman or hunter would stop to fill up his car, my uncle, who ran the gas station, would phone Monsieur Rancourt: "I've got one of them here!" And big Monsieur Rancourt would rush over to speak to the tourist and get an English lesson.

Years later, out west, I met a man who was worried about losing his French; he would drive some 250 kilometres to meet up with the Bibliobus that distributed books to francophones scattered around the region.

When I visited a school in a Vancouver suburb, I asked the young students how many of them spoke two languages. All of them put up their hands. How many spoke three languages? Almost all of the hands went up again. And now they were learning French. I asked them why. "Because we live in Canada…there are lots of people who speak French in Canada and in the world." These children, from one coast all the way to the other, who are learning a second and a third language, will grow up and do great things for our country.

I also think about Lieutenant-General Roméo Dallaire saying to prospective officers in the Canadian Forces, "Your leadership begins with your ability to speak to your soldiers, who are ready to die for their country, in both of the languages of our nation."

Canada has a rich variety of languages. In this era of globalization, let's keep that garden growing. Learning another language is like taking a beautiful trip to another's land.

Vancouver
Christopher Moore

Vancouver is the third-largest, the youngest, and possibly the most spectacular of Canada's great cities. Once a very British city—though from its earliest years it had distinct Chinese and Japanese minorities—Vancouver has been transformed by immigration. As recently as 1970, 85 percent of Vancouverites were of European origin. Today, 40 percent are neither French- nor English-speaking in origin, and almost 40 percent were born outside Canada. Immigration from China and southern Asia has made Vancouver truly a city of the Pacific Rim, in fact a city of the world, with an exciting mix of cultures, traditions, and languages.

Vancouver sprang into being as a railroad terminus and seaport in 1886, the year the Canadian Pacific Railway came to town. That year, the city of Vancouver was incorporated, burned down, and rebuilt. It grew rapidly, becoming a thriving commercial centre and the western lynchpin of trans-Canadian and trans-Pacific trade.

Vancouver, dubbed "the village by the rainforest" by journalist-chronicler Allan Fotheringham, continues to be the headquarters of British Columbia's resources industries, particularly forestry, fishing, and mining. But today it is truly a post-industrial city, thriving on financial, business, and cultural industries, as well as drawing tourists from all over the world. Its downtown is a forest of slim high-rise towers, both commercial and residential, linked to the rest of the city of 2 million by a network of bridges and an expanding rapid transit system.

Vancouver is renowned for its spectacular setting, a network of peninsulas and inlets just between the sea and the coastal mountains, adorned by the vast urban forest that is Stanley Park. Rejuvenated by the Expo 86 world's fair, Vancouver looks forward to hosting the world at the 2010 Winter Olympic Games.

50 The Avro Arrow Project
J. L. Granatstein

In the 1950s, the Cold War was at its peak, the Soviet Union had long-range bombers armed with nuclear weapons, and Canada needed fighter aircraft to defend the nation. The answer was the CF-105 Arrow, designed and developed by aeronautical experts at A.V. Roe Canada in Toronto. The Arrow was to be big and fast, a supersonic two-seater jet interceptor armed with missiles that could shoot down enemy bombers before they reached North America's urban centres and industrial heartland.

But there were soon problems. The swept-wing Arrow needed a new airframe, new engines, and new missiles. To design and build these radical innovations cost hundreds of millions of dollars, and Canada was still a small country with large defence costs and growing, expensive social programs. The Liberal government of Louis St. Laurent worried about the Arrow's soaring costs, but it kept feeding cash to A.V. Roe to develop and produce prototypes.

Then, in 1957, John Diefenbaker's Progressive Conservatives took power. The country's military chiefs warned the new Cabinet that if production of the Arrow went ahead, there would be no money for anything else the military needed. Perhaps Arrows could be sold abroad to lower unit costs? Everyone tried, but no other nation would buy the CF-105, designed to fly over the Canadian North, when U.S. aircraft, almost as good, were much cheaper. Finally, in February 1959, Diefenbaker pulled the plug, announcing that Canada would use the American-made nuclear-tipped Bomarc surface-to-air missiles to defend the nation. Instantly, A.V. Roe Canada brutally fired its work force, and its aeronautical engineers decamped for the United States. The myth of the great Canadian sellout quickly took root. Poor nationalist Dief wanted the best for his country, and he made the correct decision, but ever after he was known as the man who shot down the Arrow.

51 A Democratic Nation
David Eddie

It's something a lot of us appear to take for granted. And we shouldn't.

Voter turnout has been steadily (though with blips) declining in Canada since World War II. In 1945, about 75 percent of registered voters took advantage of their right to vote. In 2000, that number had fallen to around 65 percent.

Now, true, it's been declining in the other Western democracies as well. The U.K., France, and the U. S. have all experienced similar declines in the same period (in the U.K. it's dropped down to just over 50 percent turnout).

But it's no less a cause for concern. For many people around the world, the notion that one's government will cede power because the people have voted against it is little more than a fond notion. Ask a Zimbabwean suffering under the oppressive regime of Robert Mugabe, who considers himself "appointed by God" as ruler for life.

The strangest episode in Canada's history as a democracy had to be the FLQ Crisis, also known as the October Crisis, in 1970.

"Just watch me," Pierre Trudeau replied, when asked by a CBC reporter how far he would go to stop terrorists who had kidnapped two politicians in Québec. Although it was not wartime, Trudeau invoked the War Measures Act, which gave sweeping powers to the police and suspended the civil liberties of many people.

Now of course, Pierre Trudeau was a benign figure on the world stage. But what if he hadn't been? Many critics—most notably Tommy Douglas—felt uneasy at the precedent set by the suspension of civil liberties and the de facto declaration of martial law on democratic soil.

At the very least, this should give Canadians pause for thought: democracy is not a right, but a privilege that we've fought for and must continue to fight for and never take for granted.

Otherwise, it could disappear, perhaps overnight.

52 The Québec Winter Carnival
Roch Carrier

There is a perfect cure for Canadians who aren't the least bit fond of winter: the Québec Winter Carnival.

The first new inhabitants of this country learned a lot from the Native peoples about how to survive winter: how to eat and how to dress, what kind of shoes to wear, how to get about on snowshoes, how to skate on blades made of whittled bone, how to hunt in the snowy forests, ice-fish, transport things by sleigh, and drink deer and caribou blood to avoid winter illnesses.

This pleasure of getting the upper hand on winter is the force behind the Québec Winter Carnival. It's a party where people have fun as if summer didn't even exist! Who needs a golden, sandy beach when you can put your swimsuit on and go for a dip in the snow? Do we really need swift rivers when we can perch on a blow-up canoe and fly down a steep hill? Don't those summer streams seem a little bit boring when you are canoeing among ice floes on a wide river? And how insipid is a summer beer compared to a caribou cocktail (red wine + whiskey + a dash of maple syrup)!

At the end of January, wherever you live, run away! Bring only your warmest clothes and your thickest-lined boots and come to Québec City when it is at its wintriest! Go to the Ice Palace and the grand starlight ball in Place d'Youville. Attend a sled dog race through the streets of the Old Town. In the kingdom of Bonhomme Carnaval, you will rediscover the simple pleasure of the time you got your first skates, your first toboggan, your first skis.

Québec City is incredibly beautiful in the summer, but even more so in the snow. Riding in a horse-drawn carriage, thinking about the fact that no two snowflakes are identical, you feel like a kid again.

53 Banff National Park
Todd Babiak

For a generation of wealthy travellers from around the world, encouraged by the art deco posters depicting silver trains rushing through the Rockies or a woman in pantaloons looking out a window of the Chateau Lake Louise, Banff was Canada.

For Mexican artists schooled at the Banff Centre, British television executives pitched at the Banff Springs Hotel every June, and Australian and Québecois university students sexually educated in the whorl of the Rockies' summertime service sector, it remains a quintessentially Canadian meeting place—an engine of nostalgia.

Yet it is the conception of the national park that is its most Canadian feature.

In the 1870s, a group of rail workers discovered hot mineral springs on the lower slopes of what would be called Sulphur Mountain, in the picturesque Bow Valley of the Rocky Mountains. Resort towns in Europe and the United States were booming at the time, so plenty of enterprising men and organizations claimed to have discovered the springs.

Prime Minister John A. Macdonald interrupted the court battles and decided that no individual or corporation would own the Cave and Basin Hot Springs. Instead, he nationalized the place. The government mandated that the 26 square kilometres around the spring would be public land, protected as Rocky Mountains Park—after Yellowstone, the second national park in North America, and the third in the world.

The size of the park changed many times over the next forty-five years, but in 1930 was fixed at its current size and renamed Banff National Park.

Wallace Stegner, not a Canadian but a writer of the West, called national parks "America's best idea." The idea of a public preserve, free of the class privilege that defined European and New England resorts, democratic and protected for all, is a beautiful one—and it spread across Canada. Of course, restaurants in Banff weren't cheap in 1885, and they aren't today, but tents have always been welcome.

54 Hydroelectricity
Rachel A. Qitsualik

One can immediately glean the importance of Canada's great double-edged sword, hydroelectric power, from the term Canadians use for it: "hydro," a word many unknowingly apply to any power source, whether hydroelectric or not. No other nation produces or depends as much on hydroelectric power as Canada, and no other national Constitution has been as tested by it.

On one edge of this sword, Canada's great waters would seem to provide the perfect home for an energy source based on liquid flow. Here is the ultimate "clean" system, having nothing to do with fossil fuels, producing neither waste nor greenhouse gas. With automation, hydroelectric projects require relatively little maintenance or supervision, being long-lasting and durable. In light of burgeoning panic over pollution and oil prices, hydroelectricity must seem heavenly —especially to the energy-desperate urbanite.

The other edge of the sword, however, reveals itself in the erosion of riverbanks, destruction of fish stocks, general deforestation, and gross displacement of wildlife. That "wild" life would seem, at times, to include rural folk situated in or near the vastnesses slated for development. In some cases, displaced populations include Aboriginal cultures whose lifestyle and heritage centres on the land, whether in the form of burial sites or hunting/gathering areas. It is here, in this ancient matter of rural versus urban concern, where hydroelectricity tests all of Canada (as in the seventies conflict between Québec and the James Bay Cree).

Upon the strange and unanticipated proving ground provided by hydroelectric development, Canada's ostensible ideals have undergone continual trial by fire. Are we to accept, for example, that Canada's hunger for "progress" necessitates breaking a few eggs to gain a major resource? Or does this compromise our Constitution, under which the rights of all—not merely the majority—are protected?

55 St. Lawrence Seaway
Christopher Moore

This is not to be missed, Canadians. Go to Welland or St. Mary's Falls in Ontario or Beauharnois in Québec. Watch that lake freighter nose gently into the lock, barely a hand's breadth from the walls on either side. Watch the draining lock drop it down faster than you can drain your bathtub. That's the power of the St. Lawrence Seaway, channelling the waters of half a continent, carrying big ships almost 3,800 kilometres, from Lake Superior to the open sea, through a drop of 180 vertical metres, taller than a sixty-storey building.

Canada was built on that water route, from salt water to the heart of the continent. The Great Lakes and the St. Lawrence River were highways for First Nations travel, trade, and warfare. The first European sailing ship was launched on the Great Lakes in 1679. The first canal opened in 1783 at the Lachine Rapids. The Welland Canal first carried ships past Niagara Falls in 1829.

By the mid-twentieth century, there was grain to ship east from the lakehead and Labrador iron ore needed by the inland mills and smelters, and a million kinds of commercial cargo needing efficient transport. Bulk cargoes needed big locks and a seamless link from salt water to the upper lakes. The seaway idea was born.

In 1954, Canada and the United States agreed to collaborate on a joint project that would make the whole route accessible for large ships over 200 metres long. Most of these ships, designed only for the lakes and the seaway, never leave the inland system.

Today, almost 50 million tons of freight, half of it representing international exports and imports, move across the seaway every year, and big ships continue to ply the great waters of the continental interior.

56 Curling
Ted Barris

On the Canadian prairies, the telltale signs of a successful community have always been the presence of a church, a farm implement dealership, a hotel, and a curling rink. Indeed, competitors at the 1892 Regina Bonspiel illustrated the point: "But for one unexpected event," the *Regina Leader* reported on February 9, 1892, "everything would have passed off without a hitch ... As all the curlers were at the [Windsor Hotel] fire until five o'clock in the morning, proceedings were late in commencing...."

Volunteer firefighting aside, Canadian curlers—even the legendary names such as Ernie Richardson, Ron Northcott, Ed Lukowich, Vera Pezer, Kelley Law, and Sandra Schmirler—excelled at the game principally as part-timers. In 1875, when Toronto's Granite Club enlisted its first curlers for games on ice in Toronto Harbour, among the hobby players was John A. Macdonald.

The game was born in 1541 when two Scotsmen chose to resolve a dispute with "a tournament on ice" rather than pistols at ten paces, although Canada has definitely shaped the game since General James Wolfe's soldiers introduced it on the frozen St. Lawrence in 1759. Canadian curlers introduced such innovations as "wooden" rocks, jam tins, and even chamber pots in place of stones. Canadians brought the game out of the cold with the first-ever covered rink at the Montréal Curling Club in 1838. Curling first gained sponsorship in 1927 thanks to the W. D. Macdonald Co. of Montréal. A car dealership at Nipawin, Saskatchewan, provided four Hudson sedans as prizes during a ten-day "carspiel" in 1947. In 1968, Air Canada sponsored the Silver Broom trophy at the first world curling championship.

The Calgary Olympics first introduced curling as a demonstration event in 1988. Ten years later, at the Olympics in Nagano, Japan, curling became a medal sport, and Canadian skips Sandra Schmirler and Mike Harris won gold and silver in the women's and men's events.

57 Remembrance Day Activities
Paul Gross

My grandfather's family emigrated from Ireland to Canada, where they went to work in the coal mines of Cape Breton. Hating the life underground, they came west on a harvest train, stopping in Calgary in 1915. After the harvest, my grandfather bumped into an old friend of his from Cape Breton, a guy he knew by the nickname of Pickle. Pickle asked, "Crook," for that was my grandfather's nickname, "where is it you are going?" And my grandfather replied, "Well, Pickle, I have it in my head to go and buy myself a new suit." Pickle was buffaloed. "Why would you buy a new suit? King George will give you one for free." They adjourned to a saloon, drank a little whiskey, and then they both enlisted in the Canadian Expeditionary Force, bound for the battlefields of the Western Front. My grandfather was wounded three times, the last injury severe enough to send him home. His good friend Pickle never did make it home. These are but two men among the 600,000 who volunteered for their young country.

An unbroken line of sacrifice extends from the C.E.F. of 1914–1918 to our forces in World War II to Korea to our peacekeeping operations around the world, right up to the men and women of the modern Canadian Forces serving in the sands of Afghanistan today. The soldiers of our nation have disposed themselves with honour, with courage, and with dignity. They have represented our best qualities in the most brutal of arenas and helped define our spirit: strong, proud, resolute. We have set aside one day of the year to honour their service in the definition of what we are. Their sacrifice shines a light on where we have come from and points towards what we might become.

58 Tim Hortons
Camilla Gibb

Ah, Tim's. What would the Canadian workplace be without a box of Timbits? Or a drive to the cottage without a double-double and an old-fashioned? Or a hangover without a Tim's breakfast sandwich? And what better heralds the hope of spring than a chance to roll up the rim?

Tim's has infiltrated our lives in ways that seem essential to the experience of being Canadian. Why have we been so receptive? It's the underdog story. It's our story. A good honest tale about a hockey player and a former police constable who, in the 1960s, made a go of trying to sell coffee and donuts in Hamilton. From those humble beginnings, an empire arose, a homegrown empire that dislodged McDonald's as the number one food service operator in Canada in 2002. And now Tim's has boldly crossed the border to share the joy with our American friends.

Very proud we are of our triumph, and near-religious in our devotion to its products. The brand speaks to the Canadian in us—it's democratic, accessible, and without pretence. It's moderately priced, not garish or flashy, over-processed, or over-hyped. It's the great equalizer, where the CEO and the construction worker, the preschooler and the pensioner, all stand in the same line.

And what do our armed forces miss most when they're abroad? You guessed it. Thanks to General Rick Hillier, Tim's set up a shop in a 12-metre trailer on the Kandahar base in Afghanistan in 2006. Excellent PR. So, too, those sentimental commercials. The one where the Chinese grandfather who prohibited his son from playing hockey arrives at a hockey rink, coffee in hand, to sit alongside his now grown-up son to watch his grandson play? It gets me every time.

59 Maurice Richard
Roch Carrier

It was the day Maurice "Rocket" Richard's wife, Lucille, passed away. A group of us—a businessman, an accountant, a politician, a writer, all veteran athletes on the rink of life—sadly gathered and drank beer and whiskey. This piece of news brought home to us the fact that one day the Rocket would also leave us. Even the thickest-skinned among us admitted that the day the Rocket died, he would not be able to hold back his tears. We turned back into little boys in red, white, and blue uniforms and we were not at all ashamed of this weakness. Everyone had a reason to justify those future tears. For one, the Rocket had allowed him to dream in an unhappy childhood; for another, the Rocket had inspired the fervour to win in a life where so many people were losers.

More than twenty years after he had played his last hockey game, I accompanied the Rocket to Toronto. We were going to visit the Maple Leafs after a practice for a special showing of Sheldon Cohen's film *The Hockey Sweater*, which recounts the story of Maurice Richard and the Canadiens.

Afterwards, we walked back to the hotel. I must remind you that we were in Leaf Town, and that the Rocket had not played in more than twenty years. He lit a huge cigar. Stunned passersby stopped dead: Rocket! It's the Rocket! And they passed him scraps of paper and cigarette packs to get his autograph. Back at the hotel, his fans, both men and women, brought him gifts: cakes, homemade jam, a hand-knit sweater, a portrait of the Rocket in action.

Years later, I wrote a biography of the Rocket and finished it on the day he died. When a journalist asked me for my impressions of the Rocket, I told him that, thanks to the Rocket, the men of my generation had been better men.

60 Trans-Canada Highway
Tomson Highway

To imagine—no, to know—that you can drive from St. John's in Newfoundland to Tofino on Vancouver Island and on north to Dawson City, Yukon, and then on to Inuvik, Northwest Territories, without once stopping (except, of course, for gas) is an awesome piece of knowledge. I myself have never tried it all in one go, but I imagine that such a journey would take three weeks easy to accomplish, if not four. And to see, moreover—on a large part of that route—not one other human being in all that distance and all that time, well, that's a concept that they find it impossible to absorb in countries like France, for instance, where I live winters.

In France, such a trip, from east end to west, would take only one day—that is, twenty-four hours. And even then, you would hit villages, towns, and cities every few kilometres. Nowhere along that highway—or network of highways—would you see unpeopled land.

It never ceases to amaze me when, for instance, I look down the length—well, at least, the beginning of that length—of the Dempster Highway, that magnificent 700-kilometre stretch of road that connects Dawson City, Yukon, to Inuvik, Northwest Territories, and hits only one gas station—one!—in all that distance, well, that's enough to make you want to stand up and sing "O Canada" in ten languages.

Russia, the only country in the world that is larger than Canada, may have such highways, and I haven't seen them yet, but they would, I think, be marred by memories of the Gulag Archipelago, concentration camps where thousands of innocent people died. But here in Canada, our awesome highway system bears no such memories. It is just free, free and open-aired, free and beautiful, the way we want to keep it until death do us part.

61 Snow
Rachel A. Qitsualik

By the average teacher's definition: the answers of most students to essay questions. By the average Canadian's definition: occasional tobogganing, regular shovelling. By the average Torontonian's definition: a state of emergency. It seems strange that, although snowfall is hardly a uniquely Canadian phenomenon, it has nevertheless so bound itself to the national identity. This is true not only in the beliefs of Canadians themselves, but also those of other nations (hence, Americans who come across the border into Windsor, in July, packing skis and parkas). No one, in truth, is perhaps as comfortable with snow as the Canadian, for whom the first snowfall of the year is (mysteriously) a joy, and for whom a "green" Christmas is indeed depressing. It's a lot to make of what are essentially windblown ice crystals, and while folk wisdom maintains that one should never "eat the yellow snow," most snowflakes in fact represent ice formed around bacteria or dust (so that tickle of flakes on your tongue may be more than you bargained for).

Of course, quite a lot has been made of Inuit and snow. Canadians, in general, seem proud to "own" the snowy Inuit—and as an individual from that culture, I admit that the fact can be rather heartwarming. Inuit, perhaps justifiably, have been described as the only people who based a "technology" on snow, using it for buoys, targets, traps, weights, and (most famously) houses. But, by now, some readers are no doubt wondering: do Inuit really have so many different words for the stuff? Well, yes, and I have decided to reveal a handful herein. I thought it best, however, to
render them in English: hoar, blizzard, flakes, flurry, snow pellets, powder, freezing rain, drift, frost, whiteout, rime, hail, slush, sleet . . .

62 Canada Goose
Camilla Gibb

There's nothing particularly special about a Canada goose. It is, in fact, the most common waterfowl in North America, whose most distinguishing characteristics include a honking squawk and a boundless and indiscriminate need to defecate.

With few predators, the decreasing use of pesticides, and the accessibility of cultivated green spaces such as parks and golf courses, the Canada goose population is thriving and may well soon rival our own. They are pests, in other words.

And they're getting lazy! More and more of them simply refuse to do what they're supposed to do and fly south for the winter. But, actually, that's our fault. Why bother migrating all that way when you've got four toasty nuclear generating stations to choose from right here in the country after which you are named?

How are we supposed to know winter is coming without that harbinger of a V-formation overhead? How can we be truly certain winter is over? When the new goslings are hatched, I suppose. Here is the most civilized thing about this otherwise bothersome bird: they mate for life, and the father actually takes an interest in the children. They both guard the nest, and they buffer the goslings in a line between them when they paddle about. Okay, that's cute, but all babies are cute.

For all there is *not* to recommend it, we have adopted this bird as a national symbol. It doesn't do official duty like the beaver or the loon, but the Canada goose still reminds us of who and where we are. For obvious reasons, they're a little less sentimental about the Canada goose in the U.S., where they've had systematic culls for the last ten years. Perhaps it's time for those Canada geese living in the U.S. to consider repatriating.

63 Medical/Scientific/Technological Inventions and Advancements
Ted Barris

Ask grain farmers to name Canada's greatest scientific invention, and they might credit David Fife's disease-resistant wheat seed or Thomas Carroll's self-propelled combine. However, during the Depression, when drought and erosion created dust bowl conditions on the Prairies, a revolutionary plough design affected more than just crop yield. Developed in 1935, Charles Noble's straight-blade cultivator cut weeds below ground and sealed in moisture while leaving surface stubble as protective mulch, thus transforming the Prairies into the nation's breadbasket.

Historians might agree that Frederick Banting's and Charles Best's discovery and production of insulin to fight diabetes ranks highest among medical advances. Norman Bethune's work with his mobile blood transfusion service in China earned him heroic status there second only to Mao Zedong. And for improving the nutritional intake of Canadian infants, researchers Theodore Drake and Fred Tisdall, who developed vitamin-rich, grain-based Pablum at Toronto's Hospital for Sick Children, deserve attention. However, the development of government-run, publicly financed, universal health coverage—medicare—may top all medical advances. Who did TV voters elect "the Greatest Canadian" on the CBC? Tommy Douglas, for introducing medicare.

Canadians can brag about their technological advancements too—from A.V. Roe's supersonic jet fighter, the Arrow, to Gideon Sundback's zipper. But since Canadians' greatest adversary remains snow, perhaps our greatest achievement was the snowmobile. In 1934, Joseph-Armand Bombardier lost his son to an appendicitis attack in rural Québec because the family had no access to snow-cleared roads. Bombardier's invention of a track-driven, motorized vehicle to traverse the snow changed winters in Canada forever, giving everyone from Aboriginal hunters to medics to priests the freedom to travel in winter. What greater advance in the Great White North than an at least temporary supremacy over snow?

64 René Lévesque
Roch Carrier

When it comes to René Lévesque, many Québecers express the same kind of reverence their parents had for Catholic saints.

In the late 1950s, everyone in Québec would sit down in front of the TV to watch journalist René Lévesque explain the great issues of the day. Then Lévesque became a Liberal politician. At the time, French Canadians in Québec dreamed of freeing themselves from the yokes that constrained them: lack of education, poverty, the dominance of the Catholic Church, as well as of those who had defeated their ancestors on the Plains of Abraham in 1759.

Believing the federal government invoked the theme of national unity only to keep minorities "unimportant, docile and quiet," Lévesque could have used the unrest and frustration of his fellow citizens to his political advantage. But he decided instead to serve them. As a newly appointed minister, he began fighting corruption in public works and in the electoral system. He nationalized Québec's rich hydroelectric resources to put them in the hands of the people. He began talking about constructing vast dams, to prove to the world that Québecers could accomplish great things.

Soon though, his dreams became too big for the Liberal party, and Lévesque founded the Parti Québécois. Finding a rallying point, he announced: "A nation needs its outsiders, its violent people, its discontented, its visionaries and sometimes its rebels." The Parti Québécois was elected in 1976, and René Lévesque became premier of Québec.

Convinced their culture was threatened by the English sea that surrounded them, Québecers protested using their tax dollars to support English-language schools. But Lévesque was not afraid to tell them that "French Canadians would destroy themselves if they sought to destroy the population that does not speak French."

René Lévesque rejected that tempting extremism. He wanted to bring about his dream of sovereignty using democratic means. By respecting the people's voice, Lévesque gained the respect of many Canadians.

65 The Great Lakes
Ted Barris

Gordon Lightfoot sang about "the big lake they call Gitche Gumee" in his song "The Wreck of the Edmund Fitzgerald." He might also have referred to the remaining Great Lakes by their Aboriginal or New France names: "Karegnondi," "Michigonong," "Erielho-nan," and "Lac St. Louys." Instead, Canadians know them as Superior, Huron, Michigan, Erie, and Ontario respectively.

Whatever their names, whatever the language, their reputations for greatness remain. Together, they are the largest system of fresh surface water on the planet (nearly 244,000 square kilometres). They contain 21 percent of the world's supply of fresh water (84 percent of North America's supply). They house as many as 190 freshwater fish species, and they support the largest lakeshore human population (25 million Americans and 8.5 million Canadians) in the world. Each day, 250 billion litres of water are withdrawn (for drinking water, irrigation, and industry) from the Great Lakes basin. If it were within an individual nation, the Great Lakes economy would be the second largest in the world (with a gross product of $4.2 trillion).

The Great Lakes are home to about 35,000 islands. Superior is the deepest of the lakes, at 406 metres, while Erie's maximum depth is only 64 metres. Superior also has the longest shoreline, at 4,385 kilometres; Ontario has the shortest at 1,146 kilometres. And, as Gordon Lightfoot lamented in his song, "The lake, it is said, never gives up her dead": Superior can hold onto the same water for up to 191 years—and Michigan 99 years, Huron 22 years, Ontario 6 years, and Erie 2.6 years.

In addition to the *SS Edmund Fitzgerald*, which sank in a storm on Lake Superior on November 10, 1975, with the loss of twenty-nine lives, the Great Lakes have claimed as many as 4,000 ships since record-keeping began in 1679—ships that have foundered, cap-sized, burned, or been stranded or lost to collisions or explosions.

66 The Château Frontenac
Roch Carrier

As a small boy, I saw a photo of the Château Frontenac in the newspaper: turrets, dormers, lots of windows, and elegantly dressed guests. My parents told me that one day in 1943 a number of important men—King, Churchill, and Roosevelt—met at the Château Frontenac to put an end to the war.

Then I saw the Château with my very own eyes: it sat perched upon a cliff, with the old houses and the St. Lawrence below. I walked on the Plains of Abraham, around the walls of the Citadel. I was from a family of modest means, and I did not dare go into the Château. It was not for someone like me.

Centuries of history surround the Château Frontenac, giving it the kind of dignity that only time can give a building. On this site, Champlain built the humble Fort Saint-Louis in 1620: just a few buildings and a wooden palisade to keep watch over the St. Lawrence. The Native peoples brought furs to this spot to trade with the French, often in exchange for glass beads.

Louis de Buade de Frontenac, Governor General of New France, was a hero in the hearts of French Canadians. In 1690, backed by thirty-two ships and an army of 2,000, Sir Williams Phips demanded Québec's surrender. Not to be intimidated, Frontenac responded to Phips's messenger: "Go and tell your leader that I will answer him with the mouths of my cannons."

I travelled and studied and visited other magnificent buildings...and then I came back to Canada, across the Atlantic by boat. By then, I was the father of a six-month-old baby girl. As we came up the St. Lawrence and Québec came into view, the Château Frontenac stood out vaguely in the distance. I sat my little girl on the ship's rail, and I said to her: "Take a look at your country!"

67 Immigration/Immigration Policy
Shyam Selvadurai

Starting with the Native people, whose ancestors migrated here from Asia, our land has been characterized by the arrival of people from elsewhere. These populations, be they British, French, Irish, Jewish, Polish, Italian, Chinese, and so on, have brought cultural, economic, and religious changes that have profoundly shaped the social landscape of our country and defined who we are. A lot of the laws that make us a tolerant, open society exist because immigrants refused to assume a lower status in our country, and pushed for changes. We celebrate and take enormous pride in being a nation of immigrants, and in the mixture of cultures in our society.

Our immigration policy, with its criteria that determine who we let in and who we keep out, has been hotly contested over the course of our history. Though our response to newcomers is now very fair and our refugee policy humane and generous, there is still much debate on the continuing impact of immigration. Some of us wonder if it is necessary to let in so many, given that the "New Economy" requires a small, highly skilled work force. Some fear that the increasing non-white presence, particularly in Canadian cities, is changing Canada's character. Some immigrants, however, feel there is a lack of debate about the unfair barriers they face here, and want more immigration. In the end, no matter where we stand in these debates, we all agree that immigration is a vital issue in our country because it shapes and defines not just who we are at the moment, but who we will become in the future.

68 Environmental Conservation/ Concerns
Rachel A. Qitsualik

Considering the number of nations suffering from a paucity of environmental concern, Canadians are blessed with an atypically strong public will to preserve environmental health. But we're still foolish for ignoring the no-less-than-heroic scientists who have been screaming at us about the environment since the sixties. And we're still insensitive for allowing corporations to gut the land and pump pollutants into the skies—even after we all cried at that cool old black-and-white commercial with the Indian standing amid garbage, shedding that single tear.

But at least this grandmotherly scolding is over events that were predictable, expected of the future. No one could have predicted what would become of environmentalism once it met popular consciousness: "green" dresses and cosmetic lines, "iceberg" water, fashion shows with "recyclable" themes, frowns towards anyone failing to place cans in a blue receptacle. It seems that our response to climate change is to go high school--either that, or to go where the buffalo roam. In the halls of power, the death duels are over the usual directional flow of cash, though now dependent on the interpretation of scientific documentation. Do protocols and accords sacrifice jobs, or produce new industries that create them? Are all things free and good held hostage by suits, dreaming of oil with purse strings wound tight about skeletal fingers? Or is science playing harlot to hippie tree-huggers, manufacturing crisis in order to justify research gravy? Hunters may make one claim, scientists another, politicians and businesses yet another—but where money is at stake, all players are suspect. Behold Canada, great memetic battleground of modern Earth. We may nourish the world, once we decide not to murder it.

The Bluenose
J. L. Granatstein

It was Nova Scotia author T. C. Haliburton, the creator of Sam Slick of Slickville, who coined the name "Bluenosers" to personify his fellow Nova Scotians. The name stuck, and when a business group put up $35,000 in 1920 to build a fishing schooner in Lunenburg to compete in the newly established International Fishermen's Race, naturally *Bluenose* was the vessel's name. Designed by naval architect William Roué and captained by Angus Walters, the *Bluenose* fished on the Grand Banks in 1921 and then beat out other Canadian challengers to compete against an American fishing vessel, the *Elsie*. The *Bluenose* won handily and repeated the triumph in 1922, establishing the salt banker's reputation as the fastest fishing vessel under sail.

Forty-nine metres long, with a draft of 5 metres, carrying 1,036 square metres of sail and with a main mast soaring 38 metres above its deck, the *Bluenose* in full sail was a glorious sight, the ultimate achievement of shipbuilding in the Age of Sail. An actual working vessel, the schooner was also iconic, a powerful symbol of Nova Scotia's hard-working and skilled fishermen that would be portrayed on a 1929 50-cent Canadian stamp and on Canadian dimes from 1937 onwards.

But the *Bluenose* was already almost a relic. The age of fishing under sail was in decline, finished off by collapsing markets during the Great Depression and World War II. Although the International Fisherman's Race was held again in 1931 and 1938, and although Captain Walters' great ship won the trophy each time, the *Bluenose* had already been reduced to a showboat, touring the Great Lakes and Britain. During the war, the *Bluenose* carried freight to the West Indies, and in 1946, the proud salt banker was wrecked on a reef off Haiti. The Age of Sail had ended, and although a replica *Bluenose II* put to sea in Lunenburg in 1963, nothing was ever quite the same again.

70 Oil
Todd Babiak

The per-capita GDP of the Edmonton–Calgary corridor, the most urbanized stretch of land in Canada, is higher than American metropolitan averages and considerably higher than anywhere else in this country.

There is one reason for this: oil.

Oil is the primary ingredient in gasoline and diesel, heating oils, fertilizers, plastics, and many pharmaceutical products. And Alberta has more of it than just about anywhere else. Just one field of non-conventional bituminous sand in the northeast of the province, the Athabasca Oil Sands, has as much oil as all conventional sources in the rest of the world.

The process of extracting, upgrading, refining, and ultimately burning oil is the chief source of greenhouse gas emissions. The exponential rise in emissions in the oil sands further complicates Alberta's position in Confederation and Canada's reputation in the Western world.

Alberta has long been blessed—or, depending on your outlook, cursed—with oil. On February 13, 1947, a monstrous oil strike at Leduc Number One, southwest of Edmonton, transformed the province, and Canada. In 1980, Prime Minister Pierre Trudeau responded to the oil crises of the 1970s by creating a National Energy Program, which asserted more control over the resource in Ottawa and artificially lowered the price of oil in Canada. It was immensely unpopular in Alberta and effectively destroyed support for the federal Liberal Party in that province.

Political experts suggest that the presence of oil can have profoundly negative effects on democracy, social equality, and public institutions. Norway, an oil-producing country, sought to avoid this problem by partially nationalizing its industry and putting royalties aside in a massive fund—thus removing oil wealth and its boom-and-bust cycles from the economy.

Alberta has eschewed Norway's strategies, which were actually based on the ideas of Alberta premier Peter Lougheed and Pierre Trudeau. It may just be a coincidence, but since 1947, there has been only one change in government in Alberta.

71 1972 Summit Series
Michelle Berry

"**W**hen I saw it go in, I just went bonkers."—Paul Henderson

Ah, Canada vs. Russia. 1972. Nothing more needs to be said. I could stop here and you would still know why it was definitely one of Canada's top moments. It's that one thing you can still whisper to anyone who was older than, say, five in 1972, and actually see the memory pass across their faces. A small smile. A look of relief. Everyone remembers where they were at the time, what they were doing, how they reacted.

Eight thrilling, exciting games; we lost, we won, we tied . . . we lost, we lost again, we won, we won . . . and then Foster Hewitt's famous, "Here's another shot. Right in front. They score! Henderson has scored for Canada!" (You can still hear it, can't you?). The U.S. had the horrific assassinations of both JFK and Martin Luther King Jr., but, luckily for us, Canada's "shot heard around the world" was Paul Henderson scoring on Vladislav Tretiak. That little red light went on over the net behind Tretiak, and Canadians let out their breath in one collective rush.

During the series, classrooms emptied out. Auditoriums and hallways filled with children watching mostly black-and-white televisions. Offices shut down. This was hockey, after all, Canada's sport, and we were fighting not only for our national pride, but against communism. Both teams had travelled far, to Russia and throughout Canada, and had risen to all the challenges. Beating jet lag, tripping on the ice (Phil Esposito), losing injured players (Bobby Orr, Valery Kharlamov), and trying hard to ignore cynical and wishy-washy media and fans, the Canadian team skated through to become our heroes. They were, and are still, Canada's pride.

Team Canada defined us. We were winners. We were the nation of hockey stars. Not only did Paul Henderson go bonkers, but the rest of Canada did as well.

72 The National Anthem
Shyam Selvadurai

Though we are not a people who shout our patriotism from the rooftops, we are strongly patriotic. And every so often, we too feel the need to shout, or at least sing, our patriotism, if not from the rooftops, at least from the top of our lungs. When we stand together at school or at a hockey or football game, we are joined in that joyous way human beings have been united by song since the beginning of our existence. In that moment of singing, we are one with our neighbours, a nation.

The national anthem is often sung in both languages, reflecting our history of two founding races. The respect we Canadians pay to "others" is seen in the way we remain standing through the "other" language. The very choice of "O Canada" over the contenders, "The Maple Leaf Forever" ("In days of yore, from Britain's shore/ Wolfe, the dauntless hero came/ And planted firm Britannia's flag/ On Canada's fair domain") or "God Save the Queen," reflects our desire to be inclusive and not offend our minority citizens. Our flexible, quieter patriotism is seen in the way the national anthem has never been regarded as sacred or untouchable, but has been modified over time. For me, the national anthem is tied to the very dear memory of becoming a citizen here. That was the first time I sang it, standing beside people from all the races and nations of the world, united in who we had just become, Canadian in spirit, Canadian in song.

73 Bombardier and Bombardier Products
Christopher Moore

It's not about the skidoo any more. The whole Bombardier enterprise began with the dream of a young man in Québec's Eastern Townships in the 1920s: a motorized vehicle that would run on the snow. But The Bombardier Company, now a global competitor in aviation, railroad, and transit systems, sold off its recreational vehicles division in 2003.

Joseph-Armand Bombardier (1907–64) built his first tracked snow vehicle in 1937. Among his earliest ventures was a kind of snow-jeep, a multi-passenger vehicle for military purposes. In 1959, with small, air-cooled two-stroke engines newly available, Bombardier gave the world the recreational snowmobile: the Bombardier skidoo. Joseph-Armand Bombardier died in 1964, aged just fifty-seven, but the Canadian winter would never be the same.

Among the Inuit, snowmobiles rapidly replaced the sled and dog team as basic transportation. Across Canada, they became an essential part of farm work, still more widely owned by rural Canadians than by urban ones. Their greatest impact was recreational. By opening up the Canadian landscape for year-round recreational use, snowmobiles gave many Canadians a whole new way to experience winter. Today, one in four of the world's snowmobiles is sold in Canada. Canadians have thousands of snowmobile clubs, 135,000 kilometres of groomed snowmobile trails, and more than 700,000 registered snowmobiles.

Bombardier's success with the skidoo soon attracted competitors into snowmobile manufacture. In the 1970s, Bombardier diversified into manufacturing transit vehicles, and in the 1980s it acquired Canadair and began its expansion into aviation. Today, Bombardier is a worldwide manufacturer in the high-technology aviation and transportation fields, with annual revenues of close to $5 billion. It remains a distinctly Québécois enterprise, headquartered in Montréal and with francophone Québecers strongly represented among its leadership team. Joseph-Armand Bombardier continues to be honoured as a pioneer of technological innovation and business leadership in Québec and Canada.

74 The Montréal Jazz Festival
Roch Carrier

Oscar Peterson liked to talk about the love story that Montréal has with jazz...In the early 1950s, jazz musicians who would go on to become legends would come and play their music in the city's bars.

In 1955, a group of students from Boston came to Montréal to listen to some great jazz artist. On Sainte-Catherine Street, a crowd surrounded their bus and started shaking it from side to side. The Boston kids were having a great time. People sure knew how to have fun in Montréal! Little did they know their vehicle had come across a riot caused by Rocket Richard being sent off the ice during the NHL playoffs!

At the beginning of the summer, a wave of jazz takes over Montréal. People come from everywhere to fill the streets for a festival that has a singer at every street corner. Is it just the jazz that causes this euphoria? Well, the beer is good too!

There is jazz all day, jazz all night...It's an inclusive kind of jazz that encompasses all sorts of "cousin music," as people put it so prettily. Once at the festival, I watched an old man near the stage try to adjust his rhythm to the music, while he recalled a dance from his native country.

For this joyous crowd, often numbering in the hundreds of thousands and from all over the world, jazz is the common language. Everybody understands this voice that carries such kindness, that speaks of our happiness and our sadness, of our regrets and our loves. The skies come alive with spotlights and hold back their clouds to "let the good times roll!" Jazz unites people. The music creates an immense conversation, weaves a huge, invisible tapestry of human souls.

What a pleasure it is to explore the city on foot and to follow the music that plays in the distance.

75 Jean Chrétien
Christopher Moore

The little guy from Shawinigan, Joseph-Jacques Jean Chrétien, was the nineteenth prime minister of Canada, leading the government of Canada from November 1993 until December 2003. Canadian voters gave his party majority governments in three consecutive general elections, making Chrétien the first leader since William Lyon Mackenzie King to achieve that feat.

Chrétien was a lawyer from a passionately Liberal working-class family in Shawinigan, Québec. First elected to Parliament in 1963, he became a loyal Cabinet colleague of Pierre Trudeau and developed a reputation as a hard worker, a passionate advocate for Canadian unity, and a "little guy" who spoke "straight from the heart" (which became the title of his bestselling 1985 memoir).

Chrétien's first bid for the Liberal leadership failed, but he became leader in 1990 and led his party to power in 1993. Assisted by a divided opposition, his Liberals won re-election in 1997 and in 2000.

In domestic politics, Chrétien's greatest success was economic. After years of deficit financing, his government balanced the federal budget and delivered a string of surpluses. His greatest crisis was the near-loss of the 1995 referendum on Québec independence; he struck back with the Clarity Act, a set of rules for any future referendum. After the terrorist attacks of September 2001, Chrétien committed Canadian forces to the NATO campaign in Afghanistan, but he refused to have Canada take part in the 2003 invasion of Iraq—a very popular decision in Canada.

Amid debates about how long he would remain in power, Chrétien lost the leadership of the Liberal party to his finance minister, Paul Martin, in 2003. He retired soon afterwards and published a second successful memoir in 2007.

76 Don Cherry
Todd Babiak

The urge to worship heroes is not a particularly Canadian trait, possibly because our country was not born through war. Outside the realm of hockey—a violent, coarse, and entirely magnificent national obsession—few Canadians are universally recognized.

Kingston boy Don Cherry was never much of a player himself. He played one NHL game, in 1955, for the Boston Bruins, and toiled for the rest of his playing career in the minor leagues. Towards the end of his life on the ice, he was obliged to work as a car salesman and a construction worker, until he was reborn, in 1972, as a celebrity coach.

He was quickly called up from the AHL Rochester Americans to be head coach of the Boston Bruins. In Boston, he developed a persona that has made him one of Canada's most recognized faces—and voices. The Bruins, under Cherry's leadership, were one of the toughest teams in the league, recognized for a brutal physical style and lauded for a blue-collar ethic.

After a turbulent ten years as a coach, Cherry discovered his true calling: obnoxious broadcaster. He joined the CBC, first as a ridiculously biased colour commentator and then as co-host of "Coach's Corner" on *Hockey Night in Canada*.

In this position, he has also experimented with the role of fancifully dressed public intellectual. As feminism, official multiculturalism, and political correctness have swept through Canadian schools and institutions over the last twenty years, Cherry has been cheered—and despised—for his conservative views on ethnicity and immigration, masculinity, war, and Stephen Harper.

Cherry has used his celebrity to raise awareness for charitable causes in southern Ontario, and as a pitchman for a sandwich chain and a cold medication. In 2004, he was selected by viewers of CBC's "The Greatest Canadian" as one of the country's top ten citizens of all time.

The War of 1812
J. L. Granatstein

A by-product of the Napoleonic Wars, the conflict between the United States and Britain began in June 1812 and was fought at sea and on land, mainly in British North America. The U.S. should have had most of the cards—a distracted Britain fighting a major war overseas, a huge manpower advantage, secure land communications, and the presence of many less-than-loyal recent American immigrants in Upper Canada. But the British had advantages of their own: good regular troops and some able commanders, Native warriors, and the still-burning resentment of Loyalists who had fled the U.S. after the Revolutionary War.

The conflict opened with the skilled British general Sir Isaac Brock's troops on the attack, seizing Michilimackinac and Detroit. At the Battle of Queenston Heights, the Americans, invading across the Niagara River, were defeated, but Brock fell. The U.S. forces soon regrouped, took back Detroit, burned York, the Upper Canadian capital, and seized Fort George. The British and Canadians checked the Yanks, trying to advance on Montréal in a two-pronged assault, at Crysler's Farm and Châteauguay in October 1813. The next year, British troops stopped the invaders at Lundy's Lane in the Niagara region, one of the war's hardest-fought engagements. The last great battle of the war, fought at New Orleans after the peace treaty had been signed at Ghent, Belgium, was a major British defeat.

The War of 1812's major importance was that it saved Britain's North American colonies from the United States, thus permitting the creation of the Dominion of Canada a half-century on. Moreover, it led Canadian elites, generally unhappy with the way British leaders after Brock had fought the war, to create a "militia myth" that local citizens, almost unaided, had fought off the Americans. In fact, British regulars did most of the fighting and dying, but the myth persists.

78. Vancouver 2010 Winter Olympics
Michelle Berry

It's an odd juxtaposition, *Winter* Olympics in Vancouver, city of rain and mild temperatures. Vancouver has already won the Beauty Olympics—flowers everywhere, mountains exploding into the scenery, great expanses of ocean and forests, green space and parks—and now it will play host to the 2010 Winter Olympics. Whistler, Blackcomb, and Cypress Mountain Resort will have the snow sports, and a lot of the events will be held indoors—presumably to keep everyone out of the rain. In 1986, Vancouver hosted the World's Fair, so we know they can do it.

The event is not without controversy—environmental problems, the huge expense to taxpayers, and all the issues surrounding affordable housing. There is the women's ski jumping ban, which has more to do with sexism than with Vancouver. Even the symbol of the games, the Inuit inukshuk, has drawn criticism. The Inuit are indigenous to the Arctic, not Vancouver. Did no one look on Wikipedia?

Surely every Olympic Games has its controversy. Sometimes we forget, when we worry over the billions of dollars spent, that there is another side to the Olympics. We forget that the Olympics brings together the world. Isn't it an honour to have the world admire Vancouver the same way we do? The best athletes from around the world will compete in one of our many beautiful Canadian cities. The world will be watching and will keep Canadians on our toes (look at the difference the Beijing Olympics made regarding Tibet—it may seem small, but people are talking, people are acting, the world is observing and judging). Just debating these issues will perhaps keep Vancouver alert and responsive. Responsible. It may be a cliché, but Canadians are an incredibly proud and sensitive people. Who wants to have the world cutting Canada up? In 2010, the world will be focused on our choices. Let's hope we make the right ones.

79 Charlottetown
Christopher Moore

Good things come in small packages, and it's good to think small to appreciate Charlottetown. This is Canada's smallest provincial capital (58,000 people) in Canada's smallest province: one modern city that has preserved its character and charm by staying small.

Founded in 1768, and overlooking a broad, sheltered inlet on Northumberland Strait, Charlottetown has always been the principal town and commercial centre of Prince Edward Island and has been the capital ever since the island became a separate colony in 1769. In the 1840s, Islanders built the handsome Georgian-style legislative building, Province House. The largest building on the island when it was built, it still has pride of place in the Charlottetown cityscape.

In September 1864, Province House and the city of Charlottetown hosted the Charlottetown Conference. Amid brilliant sunshine and rivers of champagne, twenty-three skeptical politicians from several political factions in four colonies discovered the idea of building a nation. Charlottetown launched the Canadian Confederation as a realistic political option.

In 1964, Charlottetown began to promote "the cradle of Confederation" as the centrepiece of its appeal to tourists. The Confederation Centre for the Arts was opened, as both a permanent memorial to the Confederation-makers and a lively centre for arts and culture. Since 1965, 1.5 million visitors to the Centre have enjoyed *Anne of Green Gables*, Prince Edward Island's own musical classic, as part of the annual Charlottetown Festival.

Today, Charlottetown has a thriving tourism industry, government services (including the headquarters of Canada's Veterans' Affairs department and an agricultural research centre), the University of Prince Edward Island, Holland College, and the Atlantic Veterinary College, all confirming its role as the central place of island life. Charlottetown forbids new buildings over six storeys tall, and the city presents a generous mix of heritage buildings, spacious homes, and tree-lined streets.

80 Patriation of the Constitution
Christopher Moore

Okay, stay calm. This is the Constitution, but we'll try to keep it clear and simple and, with luck, no one's head will explode.

Canada has had the authority to govern itself for 150 years. But the federal and provincial governments could never agree on a set of rules for making changes to Canada's Constitution, the British North America Act of 1867. Canadians talked about it for decades, but as long as Canada did not claim the power to amend its own Constitution, that power remained with Britain's Parliament.

As part of the "No" campaign against the separation of Québec during Québec's 1980 referendum, Prime Minister Pierre Trudeau promised that if Québecers rejected separation, "We will immediately take action to renew the Constitution."

"Renewing" had to include acquiring the power to amend the Constitution. But the prime minister and the provincial premiers still could not agree. Trudeau decided the federal government would act alone, and asked Britain to pass his proposals to add an amending formula and a Charter of Rights and Freedoms. Then the courts got involved. In September 1981, the Supreme Court of Canada advised that anything less than substantial provincial support would offend against Canada's constitutional conventions.

The prime minister and the premiers gathered again in Ottawa in November 1981. It was dramatic: threats, promises, the meeting of a "kitchen cabinet," the "night of the long knives." Canada and most of the provinces—but with Québec strongly opposed—agreed on an amending formula, a Charter of Rights, and affirmations of women's and Aboriginal rights. The deal was done.

Early in 1982, Britain renounced its power to amend Canada's Constitution. In April 1982, Queen Elizabeth came to Ottawa to proclaim the new Constitution, amending formula, Charter, and all. The British North America Act, 1867, became the Constitution Act, 1982. And Canada had added a new word to the English language: patriation, "to make something part of one's own nation."

81 Good/Friendly/Polite Country
Tomson Highway

Canada is a good, friendly, and polite country. At the risk of sounding negative, at the risk of sounding like I'm passing judgement on other peoples less fortunate than us, you see wars going on in one form or another in northern Ireland, in the Balkans, in Lebanon, Israel, Iran, Iraq, Pakistan, Sri Lanka, Myanmar, Chile, Argentina, Rwanda, Zimbabwe, Jamaica, like killing like, brother killing brother, cousin killing cousin. Or at least trying to. And the basis of this killing is too frequently religion, ethnicity, land, or merely things as simple as sexual preference—as in Iran or Jamaica, where you can get hanged, beheaded, or chopped into pieces with a machete for simply wanting to love who you want to love in the way you want to love them.

Here in Canada, on the other hand, in Toronto, just for instance, you can stand on a street corner—say at Church and Wellesley or Clinton and College or Jane and Lawrence West—and you will see people of thirty different skin colours speaking fifteen different languages. And what never ceases to astonish me is that they are not killing each other. They are saying "hi," they are smiling at each other, they are holding hands, they are having babies across the borderline of race and, in the process, giving birth to a whole new race of people, a beautiful people, the new Canadian, the Canadian of the future, the Canadian who speaks not just one but four, five different languages. As a gay Cree Indian, I feel completely comfortable living in this fabulous country, like I truly belong, like I am truly wanted, appreciated, valued.

82 Victoria Day
Ted Barris

When's the official launch of summer? Despite the season's official tie to June 21 on the calendar, Canadians generally agree that summer begins on the Victoria Day holiday weekend. The occasion heralds a parade in Victoria, B.C., prompts business closures in most provinces, often sparks fireworks demonstrations in backyards, beaches, and public parks, and triggers the commencement of the annual weekend great escape, when thousands of urban Canadians dash en masse to their cabins or cottages to open them for the summer.

Alexandrina Victoria was the only child of the fourth son of King George II and Victoria Maria Louisa of Saxe-Coburg, sister of King Leopold of the Belgians. Born on May 24, 1819, Victoria reigned over the British Empire from 1837 until her death on January 22, 1901. Among the first Victoria Day celebrants were a group of Canada West (later Ontario) residents, who assembled at the corner of King and Simcoe Streets in Toronto on May 24, 1854, to cheer their queen publicly. After July 1, 1867, Victoria was celebrated as the first sovereign of a confederated Canada. Victoria Day officially became a statutory holiday (celebrated on the last Monday before or on May 24) in 1952.

Ironically, the monarch oft associated with the dour "We are not amused" retort was not as Victorian as her era's reputation. The queen's correspondence, for example, reveals her outspoken views on pregnancy, child-bearing, and what she called "selfish men who would not bear for a minute what we poor slaves have to endure." Victoria herself bore nine children in eighteen years.

Victoria's less than prudish attitudes seem more in tune with the modern interpretation of the Victoria Day weekend. Over the years, Canadians have colloquially referred to it as "May Two-Four," in part because of the associated day off, but also because a "two-four" is slang for a case of twenty-four bottles of beer.

"Cheers, Your Majesty!"

The Prairies
Tomson Highway

So you've seen the rugged coastline of eastern Newfoundland, the mighty seas that pound Nova Scotia on a windy day. You've seen Montréal and its sinful delights, you've seen Toronto and its traffic jam of restaurants that serve everything from won ton soup to pad Thai to fettuccine Alfredo to souvlaki to chicken vindaloo to shawarma. You've seen this, you've seen that. But nothing prepares you for the breathtaking beauty of the Canadian Prairies on a blue-skied August day when the wheat is at its height, the sun is at its brightest, and a wind blows gently from the east or from the west.

My father, a hunter and a trapper on the Manitoba–Nunavut border, a man who worked in circumstances of extreme solitude, used to say that there would be times when he'd come across a bog on a lonely, spruce treed island, the bog, let's say, a square kilometre of red cloudberries at the height of their maturity, and he would stop and gawk, for he had no choice, it was that beautiful. And in that silence and in that bog, he swore he could not only hear the Earth breathing—in, out, in, the sound is impossible to replicate in print—but he would see it, the lungs of the planet at work pumping air, its heart beating. And that's the feeling you get—or at least this writer does—when you see the wheat fields of Saskatchewan moving in that manner in all their golden splendour, in waves that swell and waves that fall, swell, fall, swell, fall—the lungs of our Mother, the planet they call Earth, at work pumping air, its heart beating.

Discovery of Polio Vaccine/ Salk Vaccine
Ted Barris

It took fluid in laboratory bottles, monkey tissue, and a gentle rocking motion—known as the "Toronto technique"—to make a Canadian research scientist a heroine in the fight against polio.

American biologist and physician Dr. Jonas Salk is generally recognized as the pioneer in polio vaccination. Salk studied virology and then developed an influenza vaccine for the U.S. Army. In 1952, as history's worst polio epidemic spread across North America, Salk used inactivated poliovirus cells to generate the first successful killed-virus polio vaccine. But with 9,000 Canadian children infected by polio, medical officials needed mass quantities of polio vaccine.

Enter Connaught Medical Research Labs at the University of Toronto and a Ph.D. fungus specialist named Leone Farrell, who was studying bacterial infections. Farrell had introduced the idea of gently rocking glass containers containing pertussis bacteria to produce whooping cough vaccine. Meanwhile, the lab had discovered that the polio virus grew rapidly on monkey kidney tissue in a synthetic liquid medium. Dr. Farrell managed to adhere the tissue to the inside surface of 5-litre bottles containing the liquid. Then she continuously agitated the bottles to allow the medium to generate cell production.

In 1953, Dr. Farrell's so-called Toronto technique supplied 3,000 litres of live virus for Dr. Salk's polio vaccine trials. Twice a week for nearly two years, the virus-filled bottles were packed in dairy cans at Connaught Labs in Toronto and shipped to the U.S., where the virus was killed for Salk's vaccine production. On April 12, 1955, the medical world announced that the Salk vaccine had been effective in almost 90 percent of the tests on children. Mass immunization began in Canada, the U.S., and Finland.

Dr. Salk became an international celebrity. But, aside from appearing as part of the Connaught team in newspaper stories immediately following the announcement, Dr. Leone Farrell and her contribution were virtually forgotten.

85 Winter
Shyam Selvadurai

It is hard to think of any physical reality that affects us more than winter. Winter shapes who we are as people—what we wear, what sports we play, what food we eat, our architecture, the layout of our cities, the crops we plant, the way we celebrate our rituals or modify those brought from warmer lands; winter is even responsible, some say, for our slightly austere demeanour. Winter creates a bond between all of us. We all know and share the wide variety of psychological and physical complaints related to the season, and we can readily empathize with a fellow Canadian about the tiredness, depression, irritability, joint pain, frostbite, spells of cabin fever, and dull monotony that winter brings. Across boundaries of class, race, gender, language, and ethnicity, winter is the one language we all speak, the one rite of passage we have all been through. We are never more a nation than when we are staggering against blowing snow, shovelling our walkways, or feeling our car wheels slip over black ice.

Because we are all pitted against it, winter tends to make us comradely. As a new Canadian, I was often bemused when a neighbour who had remained distantly friendly suddenly became filled with bonhomie as he or she joined me in the ritual of shovelling, sometimes even offering to do my driveway. The sports of winter, which bring such joy to so many, don't entice me. Instead, I take delight in the inside pleasures—the cozy fires, curling up on a dark winter night to read a good book, the steaming bubble baths, the smell of roasting meat or root vegetables. The season also makes me ponder the other "mythical" Canada, the vast land that stretches north. While that ice-covered realm does make me feel small and insignificant, it also fills me with a sense of romance at its mysteries.

86 Halifax
Christopher Moore

Take the short ferry ride from Dartmouth towards Halifax, and you can see the history of Halifax laid out before you in this modern city of 360,000 people.

Military history: See the Citadel atop the hill, the gun batteries around the harbour, and the modern naval vessels at anchor. Halifax was founded in 1749 to assert Britain's strength in the region. It has been a vital military base ever since.

Seaport: Consider the spectacular harbour that opens up in Chebucto Basin to the right, and the narrow entrance that your ferry is crossing. This city has always been a busy and active global seaport, from the days of wind and sail to today's container ship traffic. As Nova Scotia writer Harry Bruce put it, "Haligonians share a secret, and the secret is the sea."

Immigration gateway: Look for Pier 21, down near the railroad station. Today, Pier 21 is a National Historic Site chronicling Halifax's enduring role as a gateway for immigrants to Canada and Nova Scotia.

Centre of government: Look for Nova Scotia's provincial legislature, Canada's oldest, founded in 1758. Joseph Howe, the great nineteenth-century journalist, political crusader, and colonial premier, is just one of many Haligonians who contributed to the Canadian political tradition.

Regional capital: See the tall business towers and hotels in the centre of town. As the largest city in Atlantic Canada, Halifax has always been a centre of commerce, entertainment, and the arts, not just for Nova Scotia but for the whole Maritime region. It has long been a centre of learning, too, with four universities, several colleges, and a school of art and design.

Most of all, Halifax is a lively, engaging, forward-looking urban centre, shaped by its history but never trapped by the past.

87

Queen Elizabeth
Camilla Gibb

Her face graces our money, her profile our stamps, and her portrait our institutions. In the not-too-distant past we put down our popcorn and stood at attention for "God Save the Queen" before watching a movie in a theatre, and we're still among those to whom her Christmas messages are addressed.

While our homage to Queen Elizabeth has always felt like a quaint colonial holdover, technically she has more power over the Dominion than we might realize. Canada only gained full independence with the patriation of our Constitution in 1982. Queen Elizabeth remains our sovereign, officially recognized by constitutional law as the legal embodiment of the state. She plays a constitutional and legal role, almost wholly enacted through her viceregal representatives, the Governor General and the provincial Lieutenant-Governors.

She holds something called royal prerogative, which would grant her the power to meddle more in our business if she so chose. But she's not a meddler by nature. And besides, she likes us. She feels at home here, has toured the country extensively, sent one son to school here, and recently embraced a Canadian granddaughter-in-law, Autumn Kelly. And we, in turn, like the Queen: even more so since she had that *annus horribilis*, her dear old mum died, and she started paying taxes.

Unlike the debate about the monarchy that has raged in Australia for years, we seem quite comfortable with our association. Whenever the issue of becoming a republic is raised, the debate inevitably proves a non-starter. Let me dare suggest a reason. Unlike Australia, we straddle a vulnerable line, commonly referred to as the 49th parallel. Should the ridiculous happen and the U.S. decide to invade or annex Canada, presumably we'd have the support of the Queen's troops. Although fewer and fewer of us have an ancestral connection to Britain, as a constitutional monarchy we have a natural ally. And everybody needs a mum.

88 Hudson Bay
Rachel A. Qitsualik

Named after the post-Elizabethan explorer Henry Hudson (whose crew impolitely set him adrift in his own namesake), Hudson Bay is one of Canada's strangest geographic features, a magnetic anomaly that touches Ontario, Manitoba, Québec, and Nunavut (though its isles belong to the last). The bay is most often of interest for the number of geographical features it either combines or borders upon, such as the Canadian Shield, James Bay, the Arctic, numerous rivers promising hydroelectric power, and a lot of muskeg. As bodies of water go, it is markedly shallow, having been termed "Muddy Water" by the Cree. This is probably because it was both the beginning and end of the Laurentide ice sheet, a sort of super-glacier covering North America up until perhaps 20,000 years ago (much like modern Greenland). In other words, Hudson Bay is not part of the continental coast in the truest sense, and may in fact constitute the world's largest puddle of dirty water (made dirtier by multiple provinces dumping waste into it).

What graduates the bay from merely interesting to fascinating is the massive, semi-circular shape in its southeast side, which many believe to be an "astrobleme"—a bite taken out of the land by some extraterrestrial object, perhaps 13,000 years ago. If that is true, it likely resulted in a form of prehistoric extinction (picture a giant land sloth thinking, "Nothing interesting ever happens around here . . ."), though the effects it might have had on glaciation are greatly debated.

Since the meeting and subsequent trade between Aboriginal and Occidental peoples in the area (hence the Hudson's Bay Company), the bay has consistently served as one of the great developmental factors throughout Canadian history. Currently, it is of interest as part of the so-called Arctic Bridge linking continents via new circumpolar routes.

89 Anne Murray
Michelle Berry

What would Canada do without Anne Murray? At sixty-three, having just released another new bestselling album, *Anne Murray Duets: Friends & Legends*, Anne Murray is still, and will always be, Canada's sweetheart. Her voice (a rich contralto), her hair (still stylish after all these years), even her golfing acumen (she has a handicap of 12), and her wonderfully singable songs create a perfect Canadian package.

Anne Murray was every girl's idol in the late seventies and eighties. We sang to "Bluebird." We danced to "Put Your Hand in the Hand." We cried over "Snowbird." And, long before it was cool to have Princess Diana hair, we all had Anne Murray haircuts. Blonde (if we were lucky) and feathered. We adored her.

She's still adored. She has a list of awards, commendations, and number one records that is sky-high. Anne Murray can easily compete with anyone for the title of the most successful Canadian singer/songwriter. She's in the Hall of Fame, she is a Companion of the Order of Canada, she has multiple Grammys and Junos, several honorary doctorates, a star on Canada's Walk of Fame, and a huge list of platinum and gold records, and she even has a museum: the Anne Murray Centre in Springhill, Nova Scotia, where she was born in 1945. From adult contemporary to country to pop music, Anne Murray continues to tug at heartstrings around Canada and internationally.

What's so compelling about her is her longevity. In 1968, she broke onto the music scene: that's forty years ago and she's still going strong. What makes Anne Murray special is her naturalness. Her voice is pure and honest. Her history is largely unblemished. She just keeps singing and getting better.

A friend of mine told me that her mother recently went to see Anne Murray in concert in Toronto. She said the venue was packed with mostly grey-haired women, but Anne Murray still rocked the house.

Canadian Beer
Dave Bidini

Twelve short points about Canadian beer:

1. Lacrosse and hockey be damned: "Caps" is Canada's unofficial national sport, wherein two contestants sit across from one another, attempting to knock upturned bottlecaps off the other's beer by flicking caps from previously drained bottles.

2. Canada abolished Prohibition two years earlier than the U.S. Except in PEI, where Prohibition lasted until 1948.

3. Legend has it that, in 1535, Jacques Cartier and his men would have died of scurvy had the natives of Stadacona (Québec City) not shown them how to brew spruce beer.

4. The first commercial brewery in Canada was started in Québec City in 1668. But La Brasserie du Roy closed after only seven years to serve as a military prison.

5. Canada's first beer bottle was known as a "growler." The second kind was known as the "bomber," hence the term "getting bombed."

6. Profits from the Molson's brewery were used to build Canada's first railroad, the Champlain and St. Lawrence Lines.

7. Doug and Bob MacKenzie's dog was named Hosehead. He had the gift of flight and drank beer for breakfast.

8. Under the headline "Canadian Beer Drinkers Threaten Planet," Fox News in the U.S. blamed Canadian beer fridges—an extra fridge where beer is stored--for the exacerbation of global warming.

9. Despite the public's affinity for traditional staples, Budweiser and Coors Light regularly outsell all leading Canadian brands.

10. Citizens of the Yukon drink the most beer in Canada: an average of eighteen cases per year.

11. Fifty-two percent of the retail price of beer in Canada is taxes.

12. In October 2000, an American soldier visiting Canada was arrested for assaulting a police officer. When asked to state his defence, he admitted that he was not used to the higher alcohol content of Canadian beer. He was issued a small fine.

91 Pierre Berton
J. L. Granatstein

Pierre Berton saved Canadian history. He rescued it from academics who were determined to make history into a subject—like political science or sociology—that could be read only by specialists. History is about the stories that shape a nation, and Berton understood this. To him, narrative was the right vehicle to tell great stories, and in his more than fifty books, Berton became the nation's storyteller.

Born in the Yukon in 1920, Berton learned his craft on *The Ubyssey*, the student newspaper at the University of British Columbia. He went on to become managing editor of *Maclean's*, an extraordinarily prolific columnist at the *Toronto Star*—1,200 words a day, six days a week—a TV performer, and a man of strong views on just about everything. A devout atheist, Berton wrote columns and books that blasted the complacency of the church. He wrote frankly about sex when no one else did, and in his last TV appearance in 2004, he talked about his own marijuana use.

All this sold books, and Berton knew it, but his books stood on their own. His study of the Canadian Pacific Railway was a national event, arguably the most publicized, most successful Canadian history book ever. Well written, well researched, Berton's histories always demonstrated his unfailing talent to find the interesting details about the battle of Vimy Ridge, the Dionne quintuplets, the story of Niagara Falls—and about Pierre Berton. Berton's memoirs were a terrific read, and his account of losing his virginity as a junior officer during World War II should be required reading.

Tough-minded, certain of his own worth, Berton was one of the handful of Canadian writers who made a good living from their craft. He did it with hard work, with a gift for writing accessible prose, and with patriotism. He believed that Canada and its history were worth knowing, and he made it so.

Victoria
Michelle Berry

Take the double decker bus to the Empress Hotel for high tea—no-crust sandwiches and scones with Devonshire cream—to Miniature World to stare at the little towns and countries, to the wax museum, where a friend of my brother's had a job as Alice in the Wonderland scene. She posed all summer, occasionally blinking or smiling to startle the tourists. Visit Butchart Gardens—where you can eat salads made mostly out of flower petals—and end with the Parliament Buildings, lit up at night like a million Christmas trees. A McDonald's hamburger and orange soft drink were thrown in for the price of the ticket to "Be a Tourist in Your Own Hometown," one of my favourite things to do. I would climb to the top of that red bus and enjoy Victoria, not as someone who lived there year-round, but as an adventurer.

Victoria is odd—a bizarre British town mixed with natural beauty. The Oak Bay Tea Party (Scottish dancing and the Scrambler) on Willows Beach, the same place my outdoors club canoed beside huge seals, the same place I've seen the dorsal fins of killer whales way out in the distance. Goldstream Park, where the salmon run so thick you could (but never did) walk across the river on their backs. Thetis Lake, a weekly hiking spot where my father rescued our dog from an unintentional mid-winter swim. Horse-drawn carriages (driven by men and women dressed like turn-of-the-century stable boys) in the inner harbour, transporting tourists to the whale-watching boats. The fake-Tudor Oak Bay Beach Hotel, now demolished, which once housed a sick, orphaned baby killer whale in its swimming pool. Victoria is this combination of awe-inspiring nature and a magical, kitschy, faux-colonial city.

93 Québec Referenda
J. L. Granatstein

The Quiet Revolution in Québec, beginning in the late 1950s, shook the foundations of *la belle province* and Canada, creating new nationalist sentiments and reinforcing old ones. The man who tied both strands together was René Lévesque, journalist-turned-politician and creator of the Parti Québécois. When he took power in 1976, the charismatic Lévesque promised his people independence and sovereignty, but only after a referendum.

Lévesque took Québec to the polls on May 20, 1980, asking people to vote "oui" or "non" to a carefully worded question that proposed sovereignty-association and "the equality of nations." But it was a tough task to campaign against Prime Minister Pierre Trudeau, who smashed the separatist option in a few superb speeches. Lévesque lost, taking only 40.44 percent of the vote. "*À la prochaine,*" the saddened premier said. Next time.

Fifteen years later, and after the failure of lengthy federal-provincial constitutional talks, it was the next time. Parti Québécois Premier Jacques Parizeau ordered another referendum, proposing a sovereign Québec, but only after a formal offer to Canada had been made for a new economic and political partnership. Amazingly, many Québécois thought they could still continue to elect MPs to Ottawa and use Canadian passports and money— even if independent. The gaffe-prone Parizeau stumbled, so much so that the "oui" side's leadership was effectively turned over to Lucien Bouchard, the leader of the Bloc Québécois in Ottawa, who had made a miraculous recovery after losing a leg to a flesh-eating disease. Bouchard, as charismatic as Lévesque had been, galvanized the campaign, and the "non" side suddenly lost traction, Prime Minister Jean Chrétien and his team weakly supporting provincial federalists. The result in the October 30, 1995, referendum was a victory for the "non" side, with only 50.56 percent, the barest of bare majorities. The idea of independence was shelved—for the time being—but it has not gone away.

94 The Fleur de Lys
Roch Carrier

I was eleven years old and I was at boarding school. One evening, the priest announced: "Today, Premier Duplessis gave a flag to the Province of Québec. It's a blue flag with a fleur de lys on it. Let us pray for Monsieur Duplessis!"

We loved the fleur de lys; it was the flower of the kings of France, brought by angels from the sky to celebrate the baptism of Clovis, the founder of France, on December 25, 466. During the Crusades, French knights wore the fleur de lys on their shields and carried it on their flags. The fleur de lys decorated the coat of arms on the cross that Jacques Cartier erected at Gaspé when he took possession of Canada in the name of the French king. The fleur de lys was engraved on the lead markers that the bold French explorers planted to map their passage through Ontario, Ohio, Mississippi, Florida, and Brazil.

Since my time at boarding school, I have been moved by the sight of a fleur de lys in a stained glass window at Chartres Cathedral, which was built at the beginning of the thirteenth century. And I have lingered in front of a portrait of Elizabeth I, posing beside a coat of arms decorated with a fleur de lys.

I have seen the fleur de lys adorning houses in San Francisco and in Australia; I have seen drawings of slaves tattooed with the fleur de lys; I have seen the fleur de lys motif on Mesopotamian ceramics, Egyptian and Sasanian bas-reliefs, Mameluk coins, Indian fabrics, ancient Russian icons, African totems, Greek, Egyptian, and Germanic currency, Cretan, Egyptian, and Indian jewellery, and old Flemish and English maps.

Having flowered in so many cultures and civilizations, is it not fitting that the fleur de lys should be a force of unity?

95 National Parks
Rachel A. Qitsualik

Fortunately, those individuals in the world who are born to destroy seem roughly balanced by those who would preserve. The average Canadian should view with pride each tax dollar that meanders towards Canada's national parks system, which preserves—and thus promotes—beauty and heritage on a scale whose total area exceeds that of whole nations. As evinced by the behaviour of many governments in the world, it is not a given that such parks should exist amidst devouring humanity, and the fact of Canada's parks has enriched this nation as surely as the contributions of any of its living cultures.

In part, national parks prove the utility of the artistic mind, for their earliest incarnations on this continent were suggested by travelling poets, artists, and writers, rather than by policy-makers. They were conceived of as refuges for wildlife and indigenous cultures before the terms "environmentalism" and "biodiversity" existed, much less found common utterance. This is because they were born of the heart, before housing themselves in the head, and so to this day coax from those who visit them a sense of natural wonder. In our modern society, so full of the benumbed, the disaffected, they are often all that remains of the awe that inspired our ancestors.

It is arguable that Canada is defined by its national parks, which lie at the farthest reaches of its compass (its northernmost park being Quttinirpaaq in the High Arctic, beyond the limits of human habitation). It is further arguable that national parks define what it is to be Canadian, for they are truly most supported by public affection, on the level of the folk rather than the office. Here, Canadians are distinguished from other nations, in our love and our preservation of that which is natural and living.

96 Olympic Stadium
Roch Carrier

The stadium is beautiful on a gigantic scale. People have nevertheless made fun of it, saying that the architect was inspired by a shell, a pastry, a scorpion, or a spaceship.

Two years after Expo 67, Jean Drapeau nominates his city to host the Olympic Games. In 1970, Montreal comes out on top: it will host the 1976 Olympics ... we need to build a stadium ... Do we have enough time? Financial resources? "A deficit is about as unlikely as a man getting pregnant," promises Mayor Drapeau ...

Canadian architects are up in arms: Is the architect who has been chosen, a Frenchman, aware of the stress that harsh Canadian winters put on buildings in our country?

In August 1974, the first pillars of the colossal puzzle are anchored into the bedrock. The builders find out that 12,000 cubic metres of concrete can't be supported. They reinforce the foundation and put steel rods in the bedrock. At the beginning of the project, steel cost $200 per ton; at the end, it was up to $1,200.

The construction and assembly of the 12,000 puzzle pieces progress slowly. The workers are tired and stressed. Accidents happen far too often. In May 1975, the workers go on strike ...

Without the Olympic Stadium, the Games will not happen. What will the impact of such a failure be on Montréal and on Canada? The workers don't come back for six months. Can we get the job done on time? Impossible.

But on July 17, 1976, in an incomplete Olympic Stadium, 12,000 athletes from all over the world parade before 73,000 spectators who are enjoying, perhaps even more so than the Games themselves, a great moment in their Quiet Revolution.

Jean Drapeau didn't give up on his dreams. What a lesson for us all!

97 Juno Awards
Dave Bidini

The Juno Awards are like Canada's Grammys, only with less evil gift bags and more singers from Portage La Prairie. Initiated in 1964 and named after Pierre Juneau, Canada's former head of the CRTC, the ceremony began as a rubber chicken event at a Toronto social hall before morphing into a prime-time network television special.

Despite a promising beginning, the Juno Awards ceremony has had an awkward teenagehood, flirting with imported American performers (Aerosmith, Black Eyed Peas) and quasi-American hosts (Pamela Anderson) in an effort to sell itself, all the while remaining traditionally modest and humble in its attempt to champion the homegrown. The show has gotten better as Canadian rock and roll has improved; a few years ago in Winnipeg, the broadcast segued from the Tragically Hip playing "Thugs" to k.d. lang singing "Helpless" to Leslie Feist fighting through the show's sonic collapse in a career-defining moment. Still, the show continues to play it safe, giving your dad's favourite band (like Triumph) gobs of Hall of Fame inductee airtime while freezing out the Weakerthans, Final Fantasy, and the Dears, three bands, among several, who've benefited from the Juno's twenty-first-century cousins like the Polaris Music Prize (best Canadian album of the year) and the CASBY Awards (Toronto radio station CFNY-FM's year-end best-of log).

Nonetheless, the Junos represent that one night of the year when two out of every ten households in Canada attempt to discover Canadian music, if only to climb into their cars the next morning and tune in to radio stations who bury their beavers (a media term for hiding Canadian artists in the wee hours of the night) and slavishly pray at the altar of the worst in American and British pop dross.

0.0 Km.

7.8 Km

OTTAWA

98 Rideau Canal/ Skating on the Rideau Canal
Ted Barris

Though Canada had won the War of 1812–14, the threat of U.S. invasion still loomed large in the minds of the governors of Upper and Lower Canada. So much so that they assigned Lieutenant-Colonel John By of the Royal Engineers to devise a water route inland from the St. Lawrence River, as a secure supply line from Montréal to Kingston. In 1826, Colonel By began construction of a navigable waterway from the Ottawa River to Kingston.

One of the greatest engineering feats of the nineteenth century, the Rideau Canal extends 202 kilometres, with a uniform depth of 1.5 metres. Colonel By employed a "slack-water" system, flooding areas between the locks. Consequently, the canal route incorporated existing waterways—lakes, swamps, flood plains, and parts of the Rideau and Cataraqui Rivers—as well as 19 kilometres of man-made construction.

British stonemasons, sappers, and miners led crews of Irish and French-Canadian workers. Hand-drilling and blasting with a mixture of sulphur, charcoal, and nitre, upwards of 2,000 men per year worked on the project. As dangerous as excavation was, malaria proved a greater threat: 500 canal workers died from the disease. Another 500 workers died of dysentery, smallpox and work-related accidents.

The Rideau Canal remains the oldest continuously operated canal system in North America. In 2007, UNESCO designated it a World Heritage Site. Remarkably, as recently as the 1970s, city officials in Ottawa considered paving over the canal as an additional car expressway to downtown. Federal government ownership stopped that notion, and instead promoted the canal's wintertime use as one of the world's largest skating rinks. Its 7.8 kilometres of continuous ice surface are the equivalent of ninety Olympic-size hockey rinks.

Did the U.S. invasion ever materialize? Not with soldiers, but today American tourists by the thousands invade eastern Canada to either boat or skate on Colonel By's waterway wonder.

Aid/Help to Other Countries
Camilla Gibb

In 1970, former prime minister Lester B. Pearson chaired an international commission to look at foreign aid. The commission's report concluded with a call to wealthy nations to pledge 0.7 percent of their GDPs to the cause. We signed on with enthusiasm, and have reaffirmed our commitment over the years, but while several European countries have consistently met this target, we've never come anywhere close. How is it, then, that we have a persistent and pervasive belief in ourselves as a great aid-giving nation?

One of our inherent values as Canadians is a belief in helping others. We see ourselves as humanitarians. Though our governments may not be meeting the goal we have set for ourselves as a nation, we are giving something: some $3 to $4 billion a year, half of that bilaterally (directly to other countries, usually in the form of goods and services), the other half split between contributions to multilateral aid organizations such as the World Bank and the UN and support for our own governmental agencies (IDRC and CIDA) and Canadian non-governmental organizations.

Perhaps part of what holds us back is our awareness that aid is controversial business. Donor countries too often tie aid to their own political and economic interests. The majority of donor aid, furthermore, tends not to get to where or whom we believe it's destined, courtesy of bureaucrats, despots, and opportunists on all sides.

In this regard, we are world leaders. The UN recently thanked Canada for its progressive move to untie its food aid from any obligation of the donee country to purchase Canadian goods with Canadian aid, thereby allowing recipients to purchase cheaper, more immediately available, locally sourced goods. If we have not yet been world leaders in terms of "how much," we have at least demonstrated leadership in terms of "how."

100 Space Exploration and Technologies
Ted Barris

"**W**hy use rockets?" asked Dr. Gerald Bull at Montréal's McGill University. The Soviets had launched *Sputnik I* in 1957, the Americans *Explorer I* in 1958, the Canadians *Alouette I* in 1962. "Why not use a high-powered gun instead?" Dr. Bull figured it would be a more practical way to gather data from space. So, in 1963, his team—High Altitude Research Project (HARP)—fired a 213-kilogram vehicle from a 40-centimetre naval gun in Barbados. It soared to nearly 25,000 metres and gathered the first data about the Earth's ionosphere. But Bull's lofty dream was grounded by a nemesis—insufficient funds.

Nevertheless, Canadians have pioneered much space exploration—in financial partnership. The year after the HARP gunshot, piggybacking on NASA rockets, Canada put the first commercial communication satellite—*Intelsat*—into space. In July 1969, the American Neil Armstrong took "one giant leap for mankind" on the moon, but his lunar module touched down on landing gear built by Héroux Aerospace of Longueuil, Québec.

By the 1970s, the Canadian government had formed Telesat Canada, which employed U.S. rocket manufacturers to launch multi-purpose satellites to improve radio, TV, and phone service in Canada. In 1974, NASA awarded Spar Aerospace of Brampton, Ontario, the contract to build the Shuttle Remote Manipulator System. The resulting 15-metre-long robotic arm, "Canadarm," cost $100 million and first went into space aboard the shuttle *Columbia* in 1981.

Canadarm performed so well that NASA invited Canada to contribute astronauts for its shuttle program. In 1984, Marc Garneau became the first Canadian in space, and in 1992, Roberta Bondar the first Canadian woman in space.

In 2008, investment became an issue. The former Spar Aerospace, MDA, needed money for its earthbound business; its shareholders accepted a U.S. purchase offer of $1.3 billion for MDA's space division. After much debate, the federal cabinet blocked the sale. As with Dr. Bull's HARP project, finance had again influenced the trajectory of Canadian space exploration.

101 Canadian Elections
Todd Babiak

In the run-up to each federal election, recognized cultural figures travel across the country with their guitars and cans of Diet Coke to play songs and make speeches that might convince young adults to register and vote. Yet, for the most part, election turnout figures have plateaued in Canada.

Some of us are crazy for politics. We read newspapers and keep track of the issues, watch the debates. But most of us are too busy with other concerns, or bored. One of the most profound political divides in Canada is between those who care about elections and those who do not.

Canada follows the British parliamentary system. We have a sovereign, Queen Elizabeth II, represented by the Governor General. We have an upper house, the Senate, filled with senators appointed by the prime minister, who is chosen not by the entire country, but by his or her political party.

Canadians vote for candidates who seek membership in the House of Commons, the lower house of Parliament. Elected members need not receive an absolute majority of votes. In each riding, the candidate with the most votes wins. This system is called "first past the post," and its peculiarities are sometimes blamed for voter apathy in Canada.

Parties can achieve a majority government, and a four-year mandate, with as little as 40 percent of the popular vote. Yet newer parties, with 10 percent of the popular vote, can end up with no seats in the House of Commons.

Ontario and British Columbia have explored a "proportional representation" system, common in European countries, where parties would receive seats based on a percentage of the popular vote. But so far, citizens have rejected any proposed changes to the electoral system.

At the moment, voting Canadians seem too divided to award a majority mandate to any political party. Theoretically, this makes an election—with its attendant excitement or lack of excitement—a constant possibility.

ALTERNATE TOP 20 LISTS

1. The Maple Leaf
2. Hockey
3. Peacekeeping
4. Pierre Elliott Trudeau
5. Niagara Falls
6. The Canadian Flag
7. The Beaver
8. The Canadarm
9. Canada Day
10. Health Care
11. The Rockies/The Rocky Mountains
12. The CN Tower
13. RCMP/Mounties
14. Frederick Banting and the Discovery of Insulin
15. Wayne Gretzky
16. Ottawa
17. Parliament Hill
18. Old Québec City/Québec City
19. Diversity/Multiculturalism
20. Confederation

© Ipsos Reid
For more information on the Ipsos Reid survey,
visit www.101things.ca

as chosen by
EDUCATORS

1 The Maple Leaf
2 Peacekeeping
3 Health Care
4 Pierre Elliott Trudeau
5 Hockey
6 The Canadian Flag
7 Confederation
8 Terry Fox
9 The Canadarm
10 The Beaver
11 Canadian Constitution/
   Charter of Rights and Freedoms/
   Bill of Rights
12 Canada Day
13 Parliament Hill
14 RCMP/Mounties
15 Diversity/Multiculturalism
16 Frederick Banting and the
   Discovery of Insulin
17 Wayne Gretzky
18 The Rockies/The Rocky Mountains
19 Vimy Ridge
20 Ottawa

as chosen by
ORDER OF CANADA RECIPIENTS

1 Frederick Banting and the
   Discovery of Insulin
2 Old Québec City/Québec City
3 The Maple Leaf
4 The Canadian Flag
5 Ottawa
6 The Rockies/The Rocky Mountains
7 The Beaver
8 Health Care
9 Parliament Hill
10 Pierre Elliott Trudeau
11 Plains of Abraham
12 Peacekeeping
13 Niagara Falls
14 Wayne Gretzky
15 Canadian Constitution/
   Charter of Rights and Freedoms/
   Bill of Rights
16 Diversity/Multiculturalism
17 The Canadarm
18 Charlottetown
19 Confederation
20 Hockey

Bonus

With the launch of *101 Things Canadians Should Know About Canada*, we invited Canadians to vote for the one thing they believed was missing from the list. More than 4,000 Canadians logged on to www.101things.ca and cast a vote. They selected Aboriginal Canadians as the missing topic.

102nd Thing!
Aboriginal Canadians
Tomson Highway

Of the 5,000-odd languages that exist in the world, each has a role to play in our universal "journey." As with plants and their power to heal physical disease of one kind or another, so each language has a role to play in the power to heal psychiatric, emotional, and spiritual maladies of one kind or another. And no less is this so with the fifty-two languages that make up Aboriginal Canada.

In an essay as brief as this, there is no room, of course, to begin to even try to explain what these powers are, but at their very epicentre rests the idea that nature is alive, that it did not die as it did in Europe at that moment when mankind was evicted from a certain garden because of an act committed by a woman. In the Native languages—that there is within them, for instance, no "he" lording it over "she" with both lording it over "it," that the universe, contrary-wise, is divided into that which has a soul and that which has none--in the very structure of these ancient languages that go back thousands of years, nature, Canada, our country, is not a curse from an angry male God but a gift, a blessing from a benevolent female God, yes, our Mother, the one we never hear of in the English language, the one who was written out of history at some point in the past but who, to this day, is hidden deep within the folds of the Native languages themselves. Yes, in these languages, this land, our country is the most spectacularly beautiful garden ever conceived of, it is a paradise, a miracle, a sacred space. And that is why the Aboriginal presence in our midst is of the most vital importance.

Acknowledgements

The publication of *101 Things Canadians Should Know About Canada* would not have been possible without the hard work and support of a remarkable group of publicly-minded individuals and organizations. The Dominion Institute would first like to thank our fourteen contributors, a talented group of Canadian journalists, comedians, actors, and authors. Their insight, along with the gentle humour of Anthony Jenkins' drawings, has brought the list of 101 things vividly to life. We would also like to thank our friends at Ipsos Reid and Citizenship and Immigration Canada for their careful oversight of the research upon which our list of 101 is based. Alison Faulknor from the Institute skillfully oversaw the project from beginning to end and deserves special praise. Just as important are our editors at Key Porter Books, Linda Pruessen and Jane Warren, for expertly navigating us through the editing process. *101 Things* was generously sponsored by the Aurea Foundation, a charitable organization founded in 2006 by Peter and Melanie Munk to support Canadian institutions involved in the study and development of public policy. Citizenship and Immigration Canada and the Canadian Studies Program of the Department of Canadian Heritage provided financial support for the website and research components.

The Dominion Institute is a charitable organization dedicated to promoting active and informed citizens through greater knowledge of our country's history and shared citizenship. Visit us at www.dominion.ca to find out more about our programs.

About the Contributors

Todd Babiak has published three novels: *Choke Hold* (Turnstone), *The Garneau Block* (McClelland & Stewart), and *The Book of Stanley* (M&S). They have, variously, been nominated for the Scotiabank Giller Prize, the Rogers Writers' Trust Fiction Prize and the Georges Bugnet Award for best novel in Alberta; they have even won a couple of things. *The Book of Stanley* is in development to be a television series, and Todd's next novel is forthcoming with HarperCollins in Fall 2009. He is the culture columnist at the *Edmonton Journal*.

Ted Barris is not one of the 101 things Canadians should know. But he's covered most of them as a CBC broadcaster, newspaper columnist, author, and journalism professor. His fifteen published non-fiction books, hundreds of columns, news features, and historical documentaries include works about military history, politics, social history, sports, and the performing arts. His "Barris Beat" column and blog cover issues both Canadian and not. His writing has been recognized by ACTRA, Billboard, the CBC, and numerous veterans' organizations. He is also recipient of the Canada 125 Medal "for service to Canada and community." What could be more Canadian?

Michelle Berry is the author of the novels *Blind Crescent*, *Blur*, and *What We All Want*, which was shortlisted for a Torgi Award and has been optioned for film. She has also published two critically acclaimed collections of stories, *Margaret Lives in the Basement* and *How to Get There from Here*. Michelle taught fiction at Ryerson University, Humber College, and Trent University. She sat on the board of PEN Canada and has served on the Author's Committee of The Writers' Trust. Michelle reviews books for *The Globe and Mail* and lives in Peterborough, Ontario, with her family.

Dave Bidini was a founding member of the Rheostatics, whose twelve albums—including the 1992 album *Whale Music*, named Best Canadian Recording of All Time by CBC Radio—are considered an integral part of the history of CanRock. Dave's books include *On a Cold Road*, *Tropic of Hockey*, *Baseballissimo*, and *The Five Hole Stories*. He has made three documentaries: the Gemini Award–winning *The Hockey Nomad*, *The Hockey Nomad Goes to Russia*, and *Kick to the Head*. His solo record, *The Land Is Wild*, will be released in spring 2009. Dave lives in Toronto with his wife and children.

Born in a small village in Québec, **Roch Carrier** has spent his life travelling in Canada, on the planet, and in books. He is the author of many books, including the beloved classic *The Hockey Sweater*. He was the head of the Canada Council for the Arts, as well as Canada's National Librarian. He is presently involved with SEVEC, a body that helps young Canadians to learn about their country.

David Eddie is the author of two books: *Chump Change*, a novel, and *Housebroken*, a memoir. He writes a column called "Damage Control" for *The Globe and Mail*, and has written extensively for television, newspapers, magazines, and radio. He lives in Toronto with his wife, Pam, and three children.

Camilla Gibb is the author of three novels. Her most recent novel, *Sweetness in the Belly*, was shortlisted for the Scotiabank Giller Prize, won the 2006 Trillium Award, and was selected by *The Globe and Mail* and *The San Francisco Chronicle* as a best book of the year. She won the City of Toronto Book Award for her first novel, *Mouthing the Words*, and the CBC Canadian Literary Award for short fiction in 2001.

Born in 1939, **J. L. Granatstein** served in the Army and then taught history at York University, where he is Distinguished Research Professor of History Emeritus, until 1995. Granatstein was Director of the Canadian War Museum and writes on history, defence, foreign policy, and politics. His most recent book is an expanded version of *Who Killed Canadian History?* and he is now writing the *Oxford Canadian War Museum Companion to Canadian Military History*.

Rudyard Griffiths is co-director of the Salon Speakers Series. He is also the co-founder of the Canadian think tank the Dominion Institute and is an adviser to the Woodrow Wilson Center in Washington, D.C. He writes a regular column on Canadian issues and international affairs for the *National Post*. He has edited various books on Canadian history and politics. Griffiths serves on the boards of the Stratford Shakespeare Festival and Adrienne Clarkson's Canadian Institute for Citizenship. In 2006, he was recognized as one of Canada's Top 40 under 40.

Paul Gross is an actor, writer, producer, and director. He has won international acclaim and numerous Gemini Awards for his acting, and his directorial debut, *Men with Brooms*, broke Canadian box-office records. A career highlight was playing Hamlet to record-breaking audiences at the Stratford Festival in 2000. *Passchendaele*, a feature film that Paul wrote, directed, and starred in, was the Official Opening Night Film of the Toronto International Film Festival 2008 and was released in theatres in October 2008.

Tomson Highway is the proud son of a caribou hunter and world championship dogsled racer. A full-blood Cree, he was born in a snowbank—in December!—on the Manitoba–Nunavut border and thus speaks Cree as well as English, French, Spanish, and music. Today, for a living, he writes novels, plays, and music, trained as he was as a classical pianist by extraordinary teachers. Of the many works to his credit, the best known are perhaps the award-winning plays *The Rez Sisters*, *Dry Lips Oughta Move to Kapuskasing*, and *Rose*, as well as the bestselling novel *Kiss of the Fur Queen*.

Anthony Jenkins joined *The Globe and Mail* in 1974, where for over three decades he has drawn editorial cartoons, caricatures, and illustrations. During the 1980s, he also began writing for the paper, and continues to be a regular contributor. He has set foot in all the Canadian provinces and territories except Yukon, PEI, and Newfoundland. He lives in Toronto with his wife and two daughters.

Actor, writer, and political commentator **Rick Mercer** is the host of CBC Television's *The Rick Mercer Report*. His writing has been published in *The Globe and Mail*, *The National Post*, *Time* and *Maclean's* magazine. His most recent publication, *Rick Mercer Report: The Book*, was a national bestseller, reaching number one on the *Globe and Mail* bestseller list. Mercer has received over twenty Gemini Awards for his work as an actor and writer, as well as the Governor General's Performing Arts Award, and holds honorary doctorates from Sudbury's Laurentian University and Memorial University, Newfoundland. He is a native of St. John's, Newfoundland and Labrador.

Christopher Moore is a Toronto-based writer of history. His books include *Louisbourg Portraits* (winner of the Governor General's Award for non-fiction), *1867: How the Fathers Made a Deal* (described by Dalton Camp as "just about the best book on our history I've ever read"), and *The Story of Canada* (which *Quill & Quire* ranked among the ten best Canadian children's books of the twentieth century). He writes a column for *The Beaver* and consults widely on historical matters. His website is www.christophermoore.ca.

Rachel A. Qitsualik is an elder of the Inuit culture who grew up in the era of dogsleds and iglus (she avoided residential school, at the age of seven, by hiding behind a rock when the plane came to get her). She has a thirty-five-year background in translation and government work. In the 1990s, she made a jump to writing columns. By the twenty-first century, she had jumped to book writing, speculative fiction, and teaching. Qitsualik's writings are used as educational content in Canada, the United States, and Australia. She currently lives in Iqaluit, Nunavut, with her husband.

Shyam Selvadurai was born in Colombo, Sri Lanka. *Funny Boy*, his first novel, was published to acclaim in 1994 and won the W.H. Smith/Books in Canada First Novel Award and the Lambda Literary Award in the U.S. He is the author of *Cinnamon Gardens* and *Swimming in the Monsoon Sea* and the editor of an anthology, *Story-wallah! A Celebration of South Asian Fiction*. His books have been published in the U.S, U.K., and India, and published in translation in France, Germany, Italy, Spain, Sweden, Denmark, Turkey, and Israel.